ECONOMIC ISSUES, PROBLEMS AND PERSPECTIVES

AN IN-DEPTH ANALYSIS OF RISING HOUSEHOLD INDEBTEDNESS IN AN UPPER MIDDLE–INCOME ECONOMY – THE CASE OF MAURITIUS

Economic Issues, Problems and Perspectives

Additional books in this series can be found on Nova's website under the Series tab.

Additional e-books in this series can be found on Nova's website under the e-books tab.

ECONOMIC ISSUES, PROBLEMS AND PERSPECTIVES

AN IN-DEPTH ANALYSIS OF RISING HOUSEHOLD INDEBTEDNESS IN AN UPPER MIDDLE–INCOME ECONOMY – THE CASE OF MAURITIUS

SANJEEV K. SOBHEE,
VERENA TANDRAYEN-RAGOOBUR,
HARSHANA KASSEEAH AND
RUBEN THOPLAN

NOVINKA

New York

NOTICE TO THE READER

Library of Congress Cataloging-in-Publication Data

ISBN: 978-1-63485-782-6

Published by Nova Science Publishers, Inc. † New York

CONTENTS

PREFACE

This book is based on the research work carried out by a team of researchers at the University of Mauritius on rising household indebtedness in the island economy of Mauritius. The main aim of this book is to shed light on the characteristics of households' participating in the debt market all along highlighting their financial vulnerability. As such, their indebtedness level, financial outlays, relevant socio-economic and demographic characteristics and behaviour are exclusively studied. More interestingly, the research work also makes a comparative analysis to provide more insights into the factors that drive households into over-indebtedness. The analysis is based on microeconomic information obtained from a specific survey undertaken across 400 Mauritian households in 2014. This is complemented by information received through consultative workshops organised with relevant stakeholders from Governmental and Non-Governmental Organisations including the civil society.

Household indebtedness has always been viewed by economists as the *raison d' être* of consumption by households, especially those who are mostly liquidity constrained. It is customary for consumers to borrow against their future stream of income to finance current consumption and automatically become indebted. However, the rationality which underpins such behaviour becomes untenable when household indebtedness crosses borrowing limits and turns into over-indebtedness. Such a phenomenon has gained unimaginable proportions in both developing and less developed countries. As it stands, there exists a wide literature on household indebtedness in developed economies, especially for the UK, US and other European countries, but very limited work has been done in the context of the developing and less developed countries. Various reasons indeed account for this but the major one remains the paucity of micro-data on household financial outlays, budget constraints and indebtedness. This study tries to fill up this gap by unfolding new findings on household indebtedness from the perspectives of an upper middle income economy, that of Mauritius.

This book comes at a very appropriate time when the economy of Mauritius is becoming more services-based with a rapid expansion of commercial (retail trade) and financial activities. Thus, consumers are exposed to more products and services that may easily attract their attention and bind them to long term hire purchase contracts. This publication also provides guidance to policy makers on how to better protect consumers and their socio-economic environment. In addition, it would also help commercial enterprises including banks to better monitor and control bad debtors so as to safeguard their own long term financial worthiness.

We hope that this publication will help consumers to better understand the risks of borrowing excessively, beyond their current means even if they foresee higher future returns. Also, that they become more aware of how to better harness their income over their life cycle without defaulting.

This research would not have been possible without the funding provided by the University of Mauritius under the 'Internally Funded Research Scheme'. The authors are all grateful to the authorities of the University of Mauritius for this assistance. However, views expressed in the study and any remaining errors are solely those of the authors.

The Authors
31 May 2016
Mauritius

Chapter 1

INTRODUCTION

Sanjeev K. Sobhee, Prof

Debt is often used to maintain a stable level of consumption matched by lifetime resources, over different stages of an individual or family's lifecycle. Being indebted either formally or via informal family channels is normal consumer behavior and a certain level of debt is inevitable for most households, particularly at the earlier stages of their lifecycle. We can observe that many consumers successfully use debt to shift expenditure from one period of their lives to another (Betti et al., 2001). However, for some households, the level of debt can become unsustainable in the sense that it is at high risk of default. In this case, such households are over-indebted (Betti et al., 2001).

RATIONALE

There is growing concern about the mounting levels of consumer borrowing and the risks that people fall into arrears. Mauritius is no exception to this rising household debt problem. In fact, Mauritian households have never been as indebted as they are today (Bank of Mauritius, 2014). Between March 2009 and March 2014, the ratio of household credit to GDP increased from 13.9 per cent to 20.7 per cent. Growth in credit extended to households moderated recently, but remained robust (Bank of Mauritius, 2014). The momentum in housing credit continued to decline. As at end-March 2014, growth in household credit reached 9.1 per cent, from 17.1 per cent last year.

The appetite for housing loans may have been affected by rising construction costs and anecdotal evidence revealed that property prices may be overvalued (Bank of Mauritius, 2014). Concurrently, households have showed a preference for consumption loans, which grew by 19.3 per cent as at end-March 2014 compared with growth of 17.2 per cent a year earlier. This type of credit may constitute a higher risk for banks, particularly when they are not adequately collateralized or are unsecured. The growing switch from housing into consumption loans amid signs of lower growth of household disposable income calls for greater vigilance (Bank of Mauritius, 2014).

The contribution of this book to the literature on household indebtedness is manifold. First, to the best of our knowledge there has been no micro-econometric study on the household indebtedness and over-indebtedness problem in Mauritius. Second, this study not only deals with the static analyses of household debts but also the dynamic characteristics by considering whether household debt increases with existing indebtedness. Our third contribution rests on the case of the small island economy of Mauritius which serves as example for the African region.

Mauritius has always been considered as a model in this part of the world, for achieving an economic miracle over the past decades with good macroeconomic fundamentals, good governance and institutions as well as political and social stability. However, the country still faces major challenges. One of the key problems is the rising household indebtedness and over indebtedness which is the focus of this study. Lastly, such a study draws several policy recommendations for the government and could be also useful to the regional and international communities.

Objectives

The purpose of this research is to analyze the mounting problem of indebtedness and over-indebtedness of Mauritian households. The specific objectives of the study are as follows:

a) Investigate the Proportion and Characteristics of Indebted and Over-Indebted Mauritian Households

The study will identify the proportion of local households who are indebted and over-indebted from a given sample. The profile of these indebted/over-indebted households will be explored in terms of age, sex, education, location, occupation, income group and family size among others. We will also observe the level and types of debt contracted by Mauritian households and make comparisons across them and with existing international findings. The analysis will also encompass indebted households' expenditure patterns.

b) Examine the Income - Debt Nexus

Family debt has become in the recent past an increasingly large burden and has a differential negative impact on the livelihood of households pertaining to different income categories. Poor families, for instance, have debts such as credit card bills, student loans, medical and legal bills, and personal loans and have few assets to leverage if they are confronted by a financial crisis, such as a job layoff or long illness. In this respect, the debt-to-income ratio for different income groups will be analyzed especially in a context of debt sustainability.

c) Assess the Causes of Household Indebtedness and Over-Indebtedness in Mauritius

We maintain that the rising household indebtedness arises from a combination of internal and external factors. Households borrow for different motives namely because of consumption-income and housing-finance motives, among others. Shocks to real interest rates and income growth expectations, combined with demographic changes, the financial crisis and credit facilities in terms of the Hire Purchase Act are also considered to help explain the rise in Mauritian household debts. Trends in key macroeconomic variables will be studied with a view to assess the role of such variables in influencing household indebtedness.

d) Analyze the Financial Vulnerability of Indebted Households

Another major objective set for this research work is to identify conditions that contribute to increase the risks of default associated with indebtedness (and hence over-indebtedness). Different indicators and parameters will be proposed in the study to enable such identification. The findings will also be used to gather more information on the degree of financial literacy of households.

METHODOLOGICAL ISSUES

In this research both qualitative and quantitative methods will be applied to achieve the various objectives set using both primary and secondary data sources. A survey using a representative sample of households (400 households) is undertaken in different regions of the island, by taking into account the gender, age, education and occupation dimensions of the household. The micro-level analysis uses cross-sectional data of interviewed households.

Structure of the Book

The remaining chapters of the book are structured as follows:

Chapter 2 reviews the existing body of the literature on household indebtedness and studies that have been conducted in this area in different countries.

Chapter 3 analyzes the macroeconomic trends pertaining to household indebtedness in Mauritius using secondary data and published sources.

Chapter 4 elaborates on the methodology adopted in this research, discusses the sampling strategy and provides descriptive statistics on the profile of respondents of the survey.

Chapter 5 analyzes the financial characteristics of indebted households interviewed in the local context. Their expenditure patterns and debt levels (in absolute and relative terms) along with their financial vulnerability are investigated.

Chapter 6 covers the empirical estimation of the different research objectives of the study. In particular, econometric techniques are applied to determine the factors responsible for high levels of indebtedness.

Chapter 7 provides policy recommendations from the study and concludes.

Some Major Highlights of the Study

As reported in the analysis chapters, there are some striking features of the Mauritian household debtor that need be emphasized. It is seen that age and indebtedness follow a rather queer shape. Normally, household indebtedness drops with age as the absolute income falls, and the ability to both consume more and spend more are reduced. But in the context of Mauritius, we observe that there is quite a significant fraction of our sampled respondents who beyond the age of retirement becomes indebted.

Another facet of the highly indebted household is that debt is contracted for wealth creation. People have been found to invest massively in real assets such as purchase of additional property by contracting loans. This is done among high income households who are already property owners. The hitch here is that the indebted household may be a victim of her own action especially if net worth is used as a basis to contract further loans. Hence, an indebted household may run into the risk of becoming an over-indebted household who may lose all its long term investments in property acquisitions in case of persistent defaults.

Econometric analyzes have shown some further features of the respondents of the survey conducted whenever households indebtedness is truncated to observe over-indebtedness through different threshold levels.

Evidence in favor of a 'Demonstration Effect', which relates to a situation where a certain group of households tends to emulate the consumption patterns of its higher income counterparts, is found to characterize indebted households in this study. The effect being so strong tends to drive many, especially the younger generations of consumers into high indebtedness.

The findings on household's expenditure patterns and debt characteristics from the study are comparable to those established in high income economies such Germany, the UK and the US.

Altogether, the book has identified gaps in our institutions that remain to be addressed in an attempt to curb over-indebtedness. This is dealt with in the chapter on policy implications. We firmly believe that this book will be useful to people in the academic circles, policy makers, managers, debt controllers and members of the public.

Chapter 2

THE MACROECONOMICS OF HOUSEHOLD INDEBTEDNESS

Harshana Kasseeah

INTRODUCTION

Over the past two decades, household borrowing has grown considerably in many countries, both in absolute terms and relative to household incomes (Debelle, 2004; Rinaldi and Sanchis-Arellano, 2006). Particularly in US and Europe, demand for credit has increased dramatically leading to an equally significant rise in household indebtedness. This has been attributed to the deregulation process adopted by many countries that has encouraged higher consumption. Both developed and developing countries have eased credit ceilings which have led to laxer borrower scrutiny. All in all, access to debt both from financial and non-financial institutions, has become much easier. This deregulation process has also led to an increasing diversity of debt instruments. Credit cards debt, non-bank debt and the growing tendency of households to extract equity from the value of their house to finance consumption have led to rising levels of household indebtedness.

At the same time, rising costs, stagnating incomes and the desire to maintain the standard of living have added to rising indebtedness among households. Additionally, low interest regimes, adopted by many countries have led to falling saving ratios as a percentage of GDP and a decline in net wealth of consumers. The rise in household debt has been attributed to factors such as stable economies, financial development and legal or institutional changes. From a microeconomic perspective, much of the increase in household debts can be viewed as a rational response by households to the effects of easing liquidity constraints on households, and lower inflation and borrowing rates. Regardless of whether the increase in debt is sustainable, it has important implications.

Rising household debt is viewed as the outcome of persistent changes in income distribution and growing income inequalities (Barba and Pivetti, 2009). Through household debt, low wages appear to have been brought to co-exist with relatively high levels of aggregate demand. Claessens et al. (2010) find that household debt has been at record higher levels prior to the global financial crisis. This is evidenced in Figure 2.1, which shows that household debt has increased to record levels just prior to the financial crisis. For some countries, such as the United Kingdom, Japan and the United States, household indebtedness has fallen in the aftermath of the crisis while for other countries such as Canada, France and Italy household indebtedness is still on a rising trend.

In many countries, rising household indebtedness has been attributed to low interest rates, higher house prices and financial innovations. For instance, Bloxham and Kent (2009) find that the fall in interest rates is the major reason for the rise in household debt. Relatively little attention is given to household debt issues in the literature. Examining household indebtedness is particularly important as this helps to assess the prospects for household financial vulnerability over the medium term. The best way to undertake this task is through the use of household micro data. However, micro-level studies have not been undertaken on a wide scale given the limitations of availability of data.

From a policy perspective, there is concern about the vulnerability of households to economic shocks, such as unexpected job loss or higher-than-expected interest rates. While the household debt-to-income ratio provides an indication of household indebtedness and facilitates international comparisons, it provides a limited measure of household financial vulnerability. In the assessment of the financial vulnerability of a household, what matters more is not the absolute debt-income ratio but rather the capacity of the household to meet its debt obligations. Financial vulnerability is typically measured by the debt service ratio (DSR), that is, household debt payments expressed relative to disposable income. A financially vulnerable household is one that is required to devote a substantial portion of its income to service its debt. It faces greater exposure to negative income and interest rate shocks, and is more likely to default on its debt repayments.

More recently, the level of indebtedness has stopped rising in a number of countries, reflecting concerns about growth prospects, weaker labor markets and a tightening in the availability of credit in the wake of the global financial crisis. Indeed, the sharp rise in indebtedness in some countries over much of this decade, combined with a significant decline in lending standards, particularly in the United States, lies at the core of the global financial crisis.

This has focused attention on the possibility that the run-up in debt might have gone beyond what could be justified in terms of 'fundamentals'—that is, persistent and tangible factors—and driven instead by an increased appetite for risk and excessive optimism. By the same token, it might be that any correction could overshoot on the way down, reflecting a greatly reduced appetite for risk and considerable weakness of financial institutions in a number of countries.

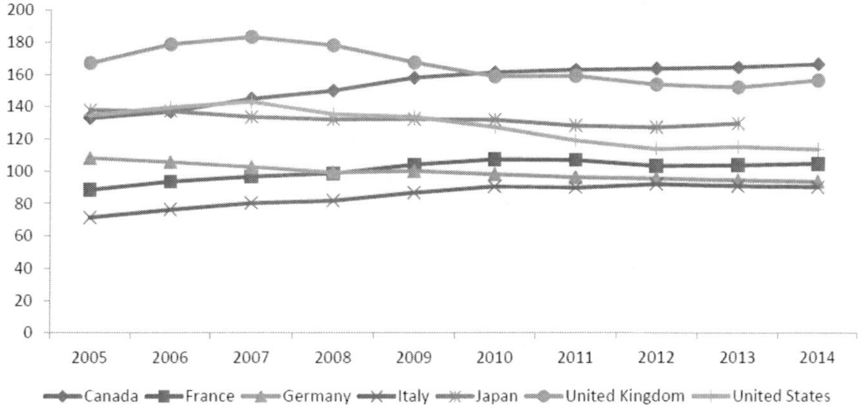

Source: OECD

Figure 2.1. Household Indebtedness, Total; % of Net Disposable Income across the G7 countries

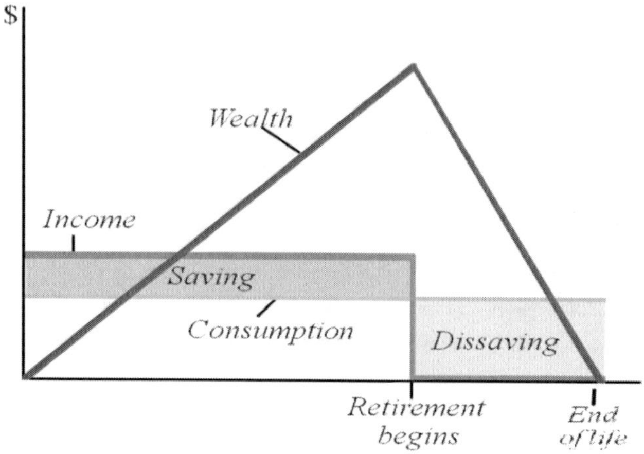

Source: Dornbusch, Fischer and Startz (2008)

Figure 2.2. Lifetime Income, Consumption, Saving and Wealth in the Life-Cycle Model.

PRIVATE CONSUMPTION AND HOUSEHOLD DEBT-SOME THEORETICAL UNDERPINNINGS

The theory of household debt and credit constraints is based on the Life Cycle-Permanent-Income model of Modigliani (1986) and Friedman (1957). The life-cycle framework is the standard way that researchers and economists alike take as a starting point in the intertemporal allocation of time, effort and money (Browning and Crossley, 2001). It has roots in the infinite horizon models of Fisher (1930) and Modigliani and Brumberg (1954).

Individuals normally have a relatively low income at the early stage and end of life, but high income during the middle of life. Hence, people try to smooth out fluctuations in income so that they save during periods of unusually high income and dissave during periods of unusually low income. The Life-Cycle Hypothesis suggests that in early life, a person is a net borrower; in the middle years, the person will save much more to repay the debt and to put aside part of the income for retirement; in the later years, the person will dissave and consume more than her/his income.

The life-cycle theory also helps link consumption and savings behavior to demographic considerations. For instance, the marginal propensity to consume out of income tends to vary with the different ages and life expectancies

(Dornbusch, Fischer and Startz, 2008). Consumption models with borrowing constraints tend to segregate consumers as being either savers or non-savers. This depends on factors such as the distribution of preferences among the population, interest rates, the variability of earnings and their rate of growth (Schmidt-Hebbel et al., 1996). In theoretical models, borrowing constraints mostly affect impatient consumers who face high earnings growth.

Building on the Life-Cycle Hypothesis, the central idea of the Permanent-Income Hypothesis is that people base consumption on what they consider their 'normal' income. Thus, they attempt to maintain a fairly constant standard of living even though their incomes may vary considerably from time to time. As a result, increases and decreases in income which people see as temporary have little effect on their consumption spending. Only when people are convinced that the change in income is permanent that consumption will change by a sizeable amount.

One explanation for the increase in the level of indebtedness is mainly related to consumers' eagerness to consume now rather than later. In today's world, consumption has increased considerably and there has been a significant change in the saving and borrowing pattern of individuals. As explained by the Life Cycle theory, households choose a path to maximize their lifetime utility and therefore apply to credit markets so as to maintain a steady living condition over the years. Thus in a period of low income relative to lifetime income, households will borrow to finance current consumption and the debt will be repaid when income is higher than the relative average lifetime income. The liberalization of the credit market as well as the development of credit scoring methods has increased access to the credit market; hence there is greater risk of financial over-indebtedness.

Put more formally, economic theory which attempts to explain household indebtedness is often characterized by the inter-temporal decision making by the rational consumer. The decision to trade between current and future income is explained by the fact that households tend to be liquidity constrained and they, therefore, try to smooth their uneven stream of future incomes across their lifetime. This is how households can borrow against their future financial resources to finance current consumption where wealth is to a large extent the main determining factor for higher consumption and the incurrence of debt (see for instance classic papers by Hubbard and Judd (1986), Attfield, Clifford and Browning (1985) and Hayashi (1985) amongst others). The inter-temporal choice is represented by the household who wishes to maximize her expected utility over a given life time subject to an inter-temporal budget constraint. More formally, this budget constraint can be expressed as:

$$\sum_{t=1}^{n} \frac{C_t}{(1+r)^{t-1}} = \sum_{t=1}^{n} \frac{Y_t}{(1+r)^{t-1}}$$

where C_t is consumption at time t, n is the expected life-time of the household consumer, r is the subjective discount rate, often equalized with the prevailing market borrowing rate on loanable funds, and Y_t is the net income receivable.

This budget equation shows that the total lifetime consumption expenditure must be exactly equal to the sum of all expected financial resources accruing to the household over her lifetime, hence considered as the wealth accumulating to the household over her lifetime. Based on the simple fact that people can borrow against their secured income streams is, a priori, a necessary and sufficient condition, to explain debt prevalence within the consumption decision-making process of any rational household.

However, one can hypothesize why some households are more indebted or over-indebted than others. There are different arguments to support this situation. First, it may refer to those households who have a more binding budget constraint than others, as they are more liquidity constrained. Their income may vary significantly and be lower conditional on the type of jobs they do. Incomes, for instance, of farmers are more erratic and unpredictable compared to those who work as government officials.

Furthermore, demographic elements may be considered with respect to the household size and the number of dependents within the family. Households who earn the same income, but have more dependents in their family, may be more financially constrained than their counterparts. Altogether, there could be a more diverse and lavish expenditure patterns across some but not all households. The degree of risks and uncertainties associated with the expected incomes over a lifetime might be underscored especially due to unforeseen events or random adverse shocks and choice of an inappropriate discount rate. Failure to account for higher inflation rates and stringent monetary policy shocks may lead to an overestimation of the present value of future stream of incomes, leading to more borrowing requirements than earlier envisaged. Changing government fiscal regimes affecting net household income may by and large explain readjustments to consumption and borrowing whenever they impact life time financial resources (see Flavin (1984) as a classic on the issue).

Rising household indebtedness has financial stability implications especially if repayment installments increase with rising interest rates and debt servicing abilities deteriorate as a result of reduced disposable income arising from job losses and inflation. Further, the household sector will be more sensitive to shocks in interest rates and household incomes, and consumption spending will be more sensitive to changes in expectations of future income. The increased sensitivity will depend crucially on the distribution of debt across the household sector (Debelle, 2004).

Increasing levels of household debt have unfortunately, not been curbed by worsening global economic situations. This has led to household sector fragility. Household fragility is a situation where households face difficulties to reimburse their household debt. This can result in non-performing loans (NPL), defined as loans that are in arrears for at least 3 months.

INDEBTEDNESS AND OVER-INDEBTEDNESS - THE EMPIRICAL EVIDENCE

While indebtedness is the result of rational economic behavior, as already explained, over-indebtedness may refer to a debt situation whereby the household is seriously financially constrained. This happens when the ratio of debt to net wealth has increased disproportionately, often overshooting the minimum threshold set for debt servicing. Households who get into this undesirable financial situation are unable to meet their regular monthly expenditure. In extreme cases, it becomes even difficult to spare enough of the income left to buy food. Errors in computing net wealth or unexpected shortfalls, temporary and chronic, may lead to such crisis situation. On the other hand, it is also the case where the concerned households have been over-consuming and over indebting themselves, for example, through hire purchase and appealing credit facilities.

Over-indebtedness creates economic, social and political concerns. Some households are simply not able to service their debt while some others are left with very meager sums after having paid all their debt obligations. In this case, household indebtedness becomes a heavy burden. In Germany, over-indebtedness has been defined as a situation where household income, 'in spite of a reduction of the living standard, is insufficient to discharge all payment obligations over a long period of time' (Haas, 2006). In France, an individual is considered over-indebted when, in spite of all his/her efforts, he/she is unable to meet its obligations coming from debt obtained for non-professional reasons. In addition, in the UK, the definition of over-indebtedness focuses on households or individuals who are in arrears on at least one credit commitment, like in paying regular bills (Oxera, 2004). Kempson et al., (2004) also focus primarily on arrears as their measure of over-indebtedness. For example, failing to meet the required minimum payment on a credit card or failing to make a mortgage repayment.

Although there is no universal agreement on the indicators which capture real over-indebtedness, some recent studies on over-indebtedness have come up with a common set of indicators, which reflect four aspects of over-indebtedness: making high repayments relative to income, being in arrears, making heavy use of credit and finding debt a burden (Keese, 2009). Bryan et al. (2010) wrote a report on over-indebtedness in Great Britain using five measures which reflect different aspects of debt, namely: being in credit arrears, experiencing debt as a subjective burden, number of credit commitments outstanding, ratio of unsecured debt repayments to gross household income exceeding 25 per cent, and the ratio of all debt repayments to gross household income exceeding 50 per cent. Similarly, Bridges and Disney (2004) and Kempson et al. (2004) focus more narrowly on whether the family has arrears on consumer debt and on other household bills as the primary indicator.

For the UK itself, MORI Financial Services (MORI, 2004) suggested four 'objective' indicators of over-indebtedness and one subjective measure in its survey, which are as follows: Individuals spending more than 25 per cent of their gross monthly income on unsecured repayments; individuals spending more than 50 per cent of their gross monthly income on total borrowing repayments (secured and unsecured). Individuals with four or more credit commitments; Individuals in arrears on a credit commitment and/or domestic bills for more than 3 months; and a subjective indicator, which comprises individuals declaring their household's borrowing repayments to be a 'heavy burden'. 'Extreme' indicators of over-indebtedness include bankruptcies, court judgments and repossession, the number and persistence of arrears, measures of household liquidity/illiquidity and so on.

From a macro-prudential point of view, it is important to mitigate the increase in household debt as this could lead to contractions in economic activities, which are harmful for growth and employment. Also, at the individual level, household indebtedness is also a cause of psychological stress and anxiety (Dunn and Mirzaie, 2013). Debelle (2004) in fact finds that the debt-to-service ratio of indebted households is highest for lower-income households. This implies that many poor households do not have any choice but to incur multiple debts and are exposed to over-indebtedness. Debt spiral or over-indebtedness means using loans to pay off other loans.

Studies by Oxera (2004), Kempson et al. (2004), Bridges and Disney (2004) and Kempson et al. (2004) have explained the term indebtedness whereby the household is unable to meet its regular financial commitments such as mortgage and utility bills or else honoring its credit card obligations. Alessie et al. (2005) refer to an Italian situation whereby some employees (essentially civil servants) benefit from a threshold equivalent to a fifth of their salary that they could exhaust in repaying a loan.

On the other hand, papers that try to address the causes of indebtedness such as Bridges and Disney (2003), Laibson et al., (2003)and Bridges (2006) attribute arrears of debt due to the cost of financing loans, in particular, the rate of interest, but at the same time the ease of acquiring unsecured loans whereby there is no need for any collateral to back the demand for loanable funds. Disney et al. (2008) have also linked household indebtedness to high income volatility and loss of employment, in which case the household's stream of income is severely impacted.

Chapter 3

HOUSEHOLD INDEBTEDNESS IN MAURITIUS: THE BROAD PICTURE

Harshana Kasseeah

This chapter provides an overview of household indebtedness in Mauritius over four decades of economic progress. Transformed markets coupled with changing households' behavior and changes in fiscal regimes have translated into higher consumption. To a large extent, the rising private consumption of households has been accompanied by a boom in borrowing from commercial banks and non-bank private sector. This chapter therefore investigates inter alia into the macroeconomic drivers and the extent to which they have influenced households' motivation towards excess contraction of credit and in many instances indebtedness in the context of Mauritius.

Mauritius is no exception when it comes to the problem of ever increasing indebtedness, particularly over-indebtedness of Mauritian households. This also calls for an assessment of the possible causes of the incidence of indebtedness and of over-indebtedness of domestic households together that can have serious economic and social consequences on the livelihood of the average Mauritian debtor. Households borrow for housing purposes, acquiring durable goods and services or financing their own education or that of their children. A report of the National Economic and Social Council (NESC, 2011) finds that "for long term projects, such as the purchase of land and housing, reliance on loans is an acceptable practice."

According to the NESC, the rules of prudence require that the monthly debt repayment does not exceed a minimum portion of the household income, which currently stands at 35 per cent according to 'normal' lending practices. The NESC report identifies over-indebtedness to take place in the following circumstances: loss of jobs, rise in the cost of living caused by inflation, impulsive purchases, breakdown of families due to death, divorce or separation; giving way to marketing temptations; the urge not to displease children; gambling, drug addiction, alcoholism, tobacco; and also ill-health leading to loss of income and the cost of meeting treatment. Over-indebtedness has major economic and social implications as the consequences include over-stress and ill-health, alcoholism, drugs, domestic violence, depression and suicide and any other related social ill. From a macroeconomic viewpoint, excessive levels of debt can have major implications for the health of the financial sector and, by extension its macroeconomic stability.

Mauritians households can, by and large, engage up to 35-40 per cent of their income in repaying a secured loan. While macroeconomic factors can be circumscribed to understand indebtedness of households, little is known about microeconomic drivers of such indebtedness and over-indebtedness. In this respect, the next section provides an overview of the macroeconomic conditions and trends of the country to provide more insights of the economic environment households evolve in. Deeper analyses are done at the microeconomic level in subsequent chapters.

Background of the Mauritian Economy

Mauritius, as mentioned earlier, is an upper middle-income country located off the eastern coast of Madagascar. Mauritius has achieved remarkable economic success since its independence in 1968 with its per capita GDP among the highest in the African region (Imam and Kohler, 2010).[1] The economy has diversified from complete dependence on sugar into textiles, then tourism, followed by financial services and recently into real estate, ICT and Business Process Outsourcing. In 2014, the contribution of the services sector to GDP was 62 per cent. As a result, the Mauritian economy now rests on many 'pillars' and is further expected to promote the development of its Blue (Ocean) Economy and Smart Cities in pursuit of greener and more sustainable development.

[1] The per capita GDP in 2014 was US $9,999 compared to $200 in 1968.

Table 3.1. Snapshot of the Mauritian Economy

	Period	*Unit*	*2010*	*2011*	*2012*	*2013*	*2014*	*2015*[a]
POPULATION								
Total Population	Mid-year	No.	1,250,400	1,252,404	1,255,882	1,258,653	1,260,934	1,262,605
- Female	Mid-year	%	50.5	50.5	50.5	50.5	50.5	50.5
- Urban	Mid-year	%	40.7	41.6	41.4	41.3	41.1	41
SOCIAL INDICATORS								
Population growth rate	Year	%	0.2	0.2	0.3	0.2	0.1	0.1
Life expectancy at birth - Male		No. of years	70	70.4	70.7	71	71.1	71.2
- Female		No. of years	77.3	77.5	77.7	77.6	77.7	77.8
Age Composition of Population								
- Under 15 years	Mid-year	%	22.2	21.7	21.2	20.7	20.2	19.6
- 15 - 59 years	Mid-year	%	66	65.8	65.8	65.7	65.6	65.6
- 60 - 64 years	Mid-year	%	4.1	4.6	4.8	5.1	5.3	5.4
MACROECONOMIC DATA	*Period*	*Unit*	*2010*	*2011*	*2012*	*2013*	*2014*	*2015*
Annual real GDP growth rate at Basic Prices	Year	%	4.2	3.6	3.4	3.2	3.4	+3.1
Growth of household consumption	Year	%	+2.6	+2.5	+2.7	+2.6	+2.6	+2.9
Gross Domestic Savings as % of GDP (market Prices)	Year	%	12.4	13.1	12.7	11.8	11.5[a]	11.4
Investment rate	Year	%	24.9	24.0	23.0	21.2	19.2[b]	17.7

Source: Statistics Mauritius

[a]: Provisional

[b]: Revised

Frankel (2014) has qualified Mauritius as an African success story whose triumph is based on sound macroeconomic policies, good governance and well-performing institutions. Yao et al. (2005) have also found that economic stability, solid institutions, political stability and efficient administration and market friendly regulations have contributed to growth in Mauritius. Subramanian and Roy (2001) too have shown that various factors have contributed one way or another to the Mauritian success story including the trade openness policy, the various preferential trade arrangements that the country benefitted from and the setting up of the Export Processing Zones that contributed to women empowerment and rising household incomes. Hence the success of Mauritius is multi-faceted[1].

Since 2000 however, the economy has suffered a series of set-backs. First, the country stopped benefitting from the preferential treatment under the Multi-Fiber Arrangement (MFA) for textiles in December 2004. Second, there were drastic reductions in the prices of sugar with the end of the European Union's Sugar Protocol, a cut of almost 36 per cent in prices. Third, rising prices of petrol and commodities further complicated matters for the economy as Mauritius is an import-intensive economy as concerns food and raw materials. In the same vein, the appreciation of the US dollar and thus the corresponding depreciation of the Mauritian Rupee has exacerbated imported inflation specially food items and health care products.

Table 3.1 gives a broad snapshot of the Mauritian economy. The country has a population of around 1.2 million with a sluggish population growth rate and the threat of an ageing population looming while female life expectancy is higher than that of males. Annual GDP growth prior to the financial crisis has been around 5 per cent on average but in the post-crisis period growth rate has been significantly lower oscillating between 3-4 per cent. In spite of this, household consumption growth has been positive. On the other hand, gross domestic saving as a percentage of GDP has been on a declining trend and the ratio of investment as a percentage of GDP has shown a similar trend.

Falling savings and rising indebtedness already ring the bell for potential hardships and degradation of financial conditions subsequently. This study comes at the right time and innovates on previous studies by providing new evidence on microeconomic behavior of households' debtors and uncovering factors that may prompt a household from defaulting. An economy that does not save is not able to invest and this harms growth. This study innovates on

[1] See also Sobhee (2004) for a review of the economic success of Mauritius over three decades or so since independence.

previous research as it relies on micro data to investigate the determinants of household indebtedness and the various motives for household borrowing.

PRIVATE CONSUMPTION EXPENDITURE AND CONSUMPTION PATTERNS

The very first element that explains the drive to indebtedness is consumption. The latter can come under two forms – namely, of durable and non-durable products. Households borrow in order to finance both forms of products, but substantially, for the acquisition of durable products, house construction, investment in education, purchase of a car or any other durable asset. Illustrated in Figure 3.1 is the trend in private consumption as a percentage of GDP over the period 1976 to 2013.

The average for the entire period for private consumption as a percentage of GDP turns out to be 79.6 per cent while that for the period 2005 and 2013 turns out to be higher at 86.1 per cent. Hence, over the past decade average consumption as a share of GDP has experienced an increase of 6.5 percentage points. Such rise is correspondingly reflected in the rising debt of households as will be discussed and illustrated in the next section.

The growth rate of private consumption is also illustrated in Figure 3.2 to provide more insights into the evolution of this aggregate and its relationship with indebtedness.

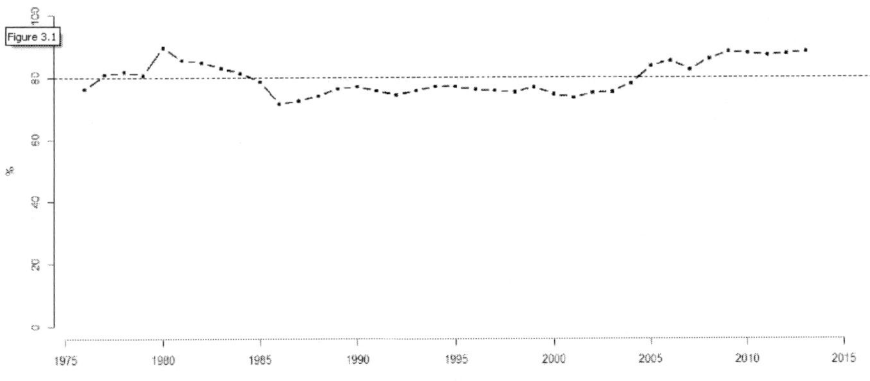

Source: Statistics Mauritius (National Accounts, Various Issues)

Figure 3.1. Private Consumption as a percentage of GDP, 1976-2013.

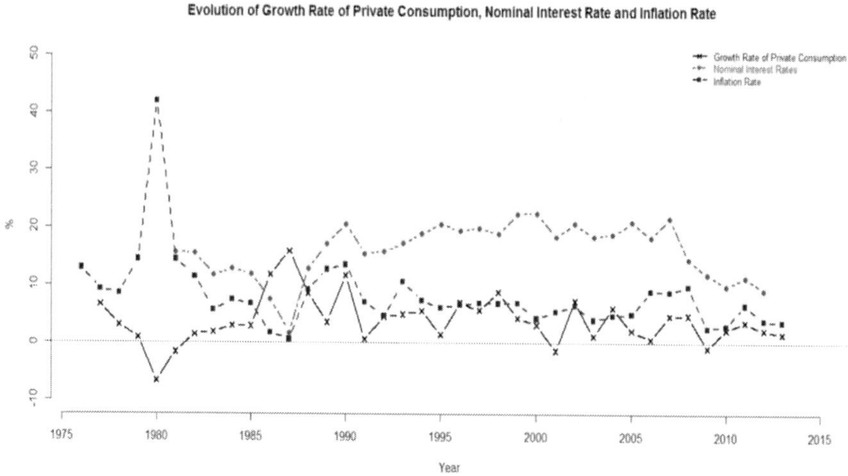

Source: Statistics Mauritius (National Accounts, Various Issues)

Figure 3.2. Growth Rate of Private Consumption, Nominal Interest Rate and Inflation Rate, 1976-2012.

The negative growth rates in the late 1970s and early 1980s could be explained by the two devaluations that occurred leading to high inflation along with unfavorable macroeconomic conditions. Subsequent rises in the growth of the consumption variable in the mid-1980s were due to the improvement in the macro-economy following the structural adjustment programmes initiated in the late 1970s. In more recent years, the drop in this variable could be attributed to the world economic recession, which resulted in a negative growth rate of consumption in 2008 with little positive recovery till 2012. Despite the downturn of the world economy and the slower growth rate of consumption expenditure, the trend in household indebtedness has continued to rise. Trends in two more macroeconomic variables, namely inflation and interest rates, which are usually associated with household indebtedness, are also discussed.

Interest rates in nominal terms have remained above 15 per cent since 1989 till 2007, for a period of almost 20 years. Such high rates could be one of the various macroeconomic factors that have led to a rise in household debt. It was only after 2007 that there has been a declining trend to motivate greater increases in the demand for loans. On the other hand, inflation has been under control since its hike in the early 1980s. Despite the fact the inflation rate has stabilized at around 5 per cent on average in the recent past, the criticism remains that the actual measurement of the consumer price index (CPI) does not reflect the reality; that is, the actual drop experienced by consumers in their purchasing power. It fails to take into account several essential food items not necessarily reflected or weighted in the basket of consumption used to compute yearly inflation.

To supplement the relationship in Figure 3.2, the correlation coefficients were also computed between private consumption expenditure and interest rates, and which, turned out to be 0.34, with inflation -0.3 and with GDP 0.99.

CONSUMPTION PATTERNS OF AN AVERAGE MAURITIAN

The characteristics of an average consumer are illustrated in Table 3.2. The information pertains to the Household Budget Surveys, which are conducted every five years.

The Average Propensity to Consume (APC) as revealed by the figures in Table 3.3 has increased. Whether mean income and expenditure or median income and expenditure methods are used, it is found that APC has increased significantly over the past decade. However, the rise is more significant when mean is used as a measure of central tendency where the rise is from 0.80 to 0.97 from 2001/02 to 2012. The rising APC indicates that consumers are spending a much higher proportion of their income on goods and services. Over the same period, it is worth noting that the Marginal Propensity to Consume (MPC) which refers to the additional amount spent by the consumer out of additional income has also shown significant increases from both statistical methods. Using the mean, MPC is found to have increased from 0.90 to 1.52 while using the median; the rise is from 0.89 to 1.08 over the past decade. The values of MPC exceeding 1 clearly indicate that households have been significantly dissaving and/or borrowing to finance consumption expenditure. The rise in MPC synonymously reflects more binding financial constraints.

In addition to the above trends in Table 3.3, which explain why more households are driven into debt, it is equally important to note that income inequality has also increased over the period considered. The Gini coefficient increased from 0.371 in 2001/02 to 0.413 in 2012, which is also reflected in the proportion of households earning less than both the mean and median income. These findings could indicate that more households are facing tighter budget constraints and might have recourse to higher demand for loans and credit purchases. This could also potentially include those who earn a reasonably "high" income.

Table 3.2. Household Expenditure and Income Inequality

ITEM	*2001/02*	*2006/07*	*2012*
Household Income			
Average monthly income (Rs)	14232	19083	23960
Median monthly income (Rs)	11150	14640	21790
% of households earning less than 50% of ½ median monthly income	13.1	14.3	17.1
Gini Coefficient	0.371	0.388	0.413
Household Consumption Expenditure			
Average monthly expenditure (Rs)	11390	15770	23200
Median monthly expenditure (Rs)	8154	11270	18550
% of households earning less than 50% of the monthly median expenditure	12.3	12.0	13.5

Source: SM (Mauritius in Figures, 2012)

Table 3.3. Evolution of the Average Propensity to Consume (APC), 2001 -2012

Year	*Based on Average Consumer Income and Expenditure*	*Based on Median Income and Expenditure*
2001/02	0.80	0.73
2005/06	0.83	0.77
2011/12	0.97	0.85

Source: Authors' Computation

Table 3.4. Household Budget Surveys 2001/02, 2006/07 & 2012

ITEM	*2001/02*	*2006/07*	*2012*
Breakdown of Monthly Household Expenditure as a % of Total Expenditure			
Food & non-alcoholic beverages	31.6	28.5	27.3
Alcoholic beverages & tobacco	9.1	9.2	9.6
Clothing & footwear	6.4	5.1	4.5
Housing & utilities	9.3	13.1	12.0
Furnishing, household equipment & routine household maintenance	6.0	6.5	6.1
Health	2.5	3.0	3.9
Transport	12.6	14.6	15.2
Communication	3.3	3.6	3.9
Recreation & culture	4.6	4.8	4.3
Education	3.7	3.2	4.5
Restaurants & hotels	6.1	4.3	4.6
Miscellaneous goods & services	4.8	4.0	4.1

Source: Statistics Mauritius (Mauritius in Figures, 2012)

To reconcile the increasing expenditure of households, a breakdown of the expenditure patterns of an average household is provided in Table 3.4. While the biggest proportion of household expenditure is on 'Food and non-alcoholic beverages', to the tune of 27.3 per cent, 'Transport' absorbs 15.2 per cent, followed by 'Housing and Utilities' which represents 12.0 per cent of overall household expenditure in 2012. Also, worth noting is the expenditure on 'Alcoholic beverages and tobacco' which accounts almost 10 per cent and has been continuously rising since 2001/02.

Characteristics and Trend of Household Indebtedness

As at end-March 2011, household debt in Mauritius reached 18.3 per cent of GDP, up from 16.8 per cent as at end-March 2010. This may point to increased household vulnerability and may warrant closer monitoring of the household sector, particularly with regard to debt repayment capacity (Financial Stability Report, 2011). Credit to households represented 18.2 per cent of GDP as at March 2012, up by 1.4 percentage points compared to the corresponding period of the previous year. Household credit has for the past quarters maintained, on average, more than 20 per cent share in total credit to the private sector, thus indicating the importance of households in banks' credit portfolio. The year-on-year growth rate of household credit stood at 17.6 per cent as at end-June 2012 up from 15.6 per cent as at end-June 2011 (Financial Stability Report, 2012). Consequently, gross national saving as a percentage of GDP has been on a continuous declining trend.

The Mauritian household indebtedness arises from borrowings from depository corporations (including a state-owned housing company), insurance companies, hire purchase companies and credit finance companies. Households also remain among the largest borrower groups in the banking sector, with household funding mainly channeled to asset-building. The investments as regards to real estate are well ingrained in the population. However, it is not only the real estate loans that have resulted in the high debt levels but also personal and business loans used to finance the costs of education or purchase of vehicles.

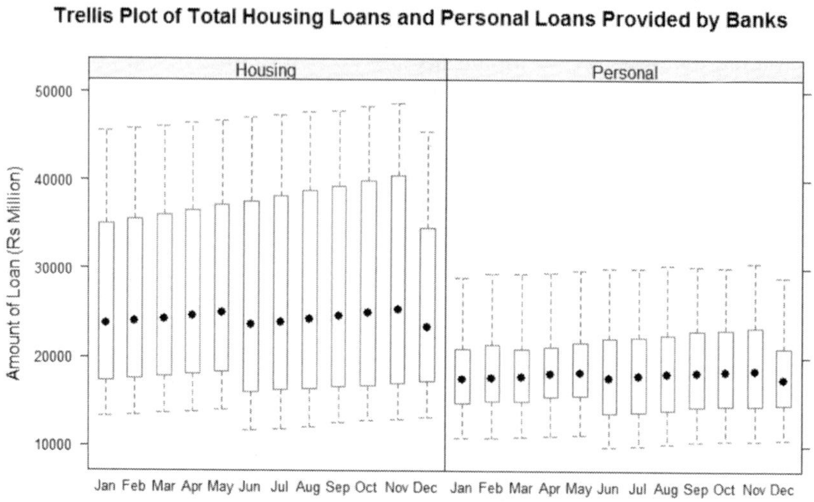

Source: Bank of Mauritius

Figure 3.5. Total Housing Loans and Personal Loans Provided by Banks.

Figure 3.5 depicts a trellis plot which contains the box and whisker plots for monthly housing and personal borrowings over the years 1995 to 2014. It is observed that loans for housing purposes exceed loans for personal purposes. In particular, the median amount of loans taken for both personal and housing purposes are higher in May and November compared to other months. A growing proportion of Mauritian household debt is also incurred to fund consumption. Borrowings to fund consumption attract higher interest rates than mortgages as the borrowing is unsecured and the risk to lenders is greater. Many families seem to be trapped in a vicious circle. They have borrowed to enjoy higher consumption previously and to maintain these levels they have to borrow even more. Growth in consumption spending therefore inevitably slows and indeed acts as a brake on future economic growth. When households try to reduce their debt by cutting consumption spending below what it was in the past, the short-term effect on growth is more severe.

At the end of March 2010, housing finance accounted for 56.9 per cent of total household loans extended by banks while the remaining share was for consumption purposes, which also include loans for the purchase of assets. At the end of September 2010, housing loans stood at 57.3 per cent while personal advances on credit cards stood at 39.4 per cent. Within consumption loans, credit card advances amounted to 8.5 per cent. Mortgage loans accounted for 59.7 per cent of total household credit as at end-June 2012, while the remainder was extended as consumption loans. For the same period, the share of housing loans in total household loans increased to 59.7 per cent. This is indicative that indebtedness of households is towards building of assets (Financial Stability Report, 2012). In addition, the recent financial crisis has shown that household financial fragility may have important financial stability implications as, despite the existence of collaterals and lenders legal protection, personal bankruptcy is costly for lenders.

Household credit-to-GDP ratio increased rapidly between mid-2008 to early 2013. The household sector witnessed rapid growth over the past years and represents a key component of banks' balance sheets. Between March 2009 and March 2014, the ratio of household credit to GDP increased from 13.9 per cent to 20.7 per cent. Households have shown a preference for consumption loans, which grew by 19.3 per cent as at end-March 2014 compared with growth of 17.2 per cent a year earlier. This type of credit may constitute a higher risk for banks, particularly when they are not adequately collateralized or unsecured.

Non-Performing Loans (NPL) in the personal sector, as an indicator of the quality of consumption loans remained high despite a drop to 9.1 per cent as at end-March 2014, from 9.8 per cent a year earlier. The growing switch from housing into consumption amid signs of lower growth of household disposable income calls for greater vigilance. The implementation of macro prudential measures since January 2014 is expected to reinforce the resilience of the banking sector to potential risks that may arise from the housing market (Financial Stability Report, 2014).

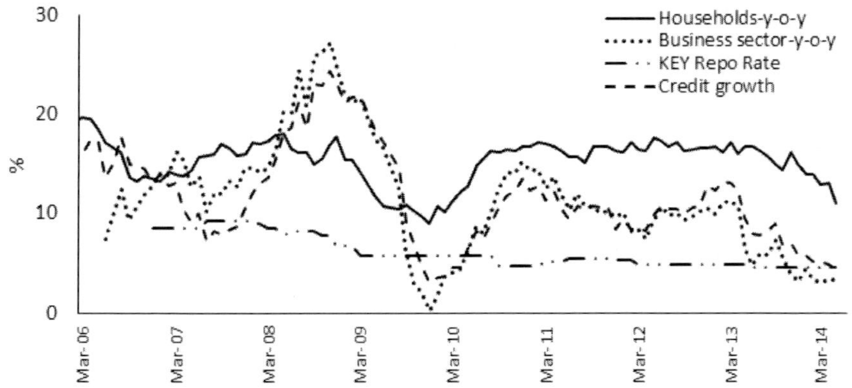

Source: Bank of Mauritius, Financial Stability Reports

Figure 3.6. Credit Allocation, 2006-2014.

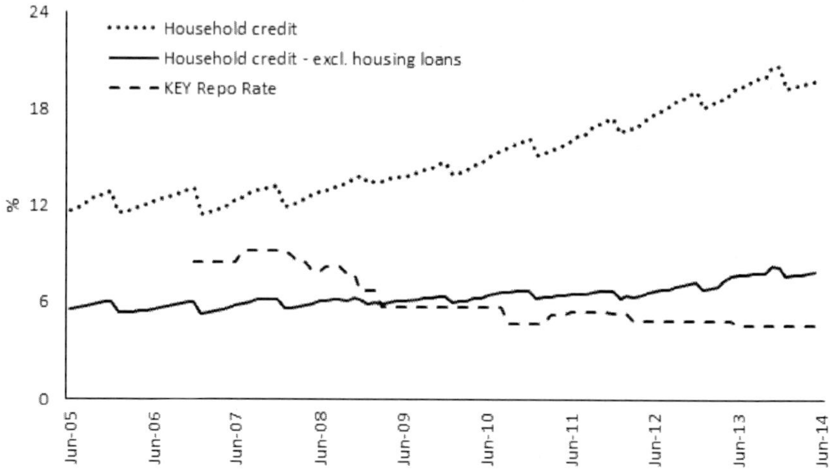

Source: Bank of Mauritius, Financial Stability Report[2], 2014

Figure 3.7. Household Credit in Percentages, 2005-2014.

Table 3.5. Decomposing Household Credit into Housing and Non-Housing Credit

Household credit-to-GDP	*Household credit (less housing loans)-to-GDP*	*Household credit (housing loans)-to-GDP*
12.9% in Jun-08	6.1% in Jun-08	6.8% in Jun-08
20.7% in Dec-13	8.3% in Dec-13	12.4% in Dec-13
19.8% in May-14	7.9% in May-14	11.9% in May-14

Source: Bank of Mauritius

However, the ratio of household credit adjusted for housing loans to GDP did not register the same rapid increase. As such, the indebtedness of household will cover a protracted period given the nature of housing loans, but as income rises the incidence on consumption will tend to be mitigated, other things remaining unchanged.

According to the BoM, the correlation between housing loans and the low interest rate environment appears very strong. During the period considered, most of the increase in household credit went towards financing housing loans. Besides banks, other financial institutions also extend credit to households,

[2] The Key Repo Rate is the policy interest rate of the central bank, that is the Bank of Mauritius, and which indicates the monetary policy stance of the Bank.

such as non-bank deposit taking institutions (NBDTIs), insurance companies, credit unions, hire purchase companies, etc.

As at end-December 2013, NBDTIs had granted Rs29 billion to the *Personal* sector while banks has extended Rs 76 billion to the household sector. *(No adjustments were made for micro and small enterprises contracting loans as households.)* Altogether, banks and NBDTIs have extended aggregate credit of Rs105 billion to households, representing 27per cent of GDP. To mitigate risks stemming from credit concentration in specific sectors, the Bank has imposed regulatory limits on the total credit that can be granted to the *Personal* sector by banks. The limit will be implemented in a phased manner starting from 15per cent as from 1 July 2014 and 12.5per cent as from 1 July 2015. Loan to Value (LTV) ratios were also introduced by the Bank. Household consumption growth in Mauritius has declined from 6.5 per cent on average over the five-year period 2005-2008 to 2.5 on an average over the subsequent five-year period 2009-2013. This decline may represent a 'permanent' downward shift in consumption, which could be because of over-indebtedness of households.

Hence, based on the analyses carried out in this chapter, it is yet to be determined what could have motivated households into more loans and greater indebtedness, leading potentially to over indebtedness, among some households in recent years. While the macroeconomic aspects of indebtedness as explored in this chapter may provide an overview of the possible causes of indebtedness, it does not necessarily convey the very elements that have dragged households into severe indebtedness. Some of these issues can only be addressed using microeconomic data and individual household surveys. The next chapter attempts to address these issues.

Chapter 4

SURVEY METHODS AND PROFILE OF RESPONDENTS

Ruben Thoplan

INTRODUCTION

This chapter sets out the survey methods used in the study and investigates the profile of respondents in the sample. The survey models the different research questions designed for the purpose of this study namely the participation of Mauritian households in the debt market and the financial vulnerability of indebted and over-indebted families.

RESEARCH METHODOLOGY

A survey has been carried out among 400 households. The questionnaire was designed originally in English and then translated into the native language (Creole) to facilitate data collection. Several factors, including financial costs, time and the desired level of precision were taken into consideration while devising the sampling strategy and methodology of the study.

SAMPLING DESIGN AND SELECTION

The sample of 400 households was randomly selected through a 2 stage sampling procedure. 30 enumeration areas were randomly selected from the list of enumeration areas developed by Statistics Mauritius using the Probability Proportional to Size (PPS) sampling method during the first stage. A sample of 400 households was then selected within each enumeration area in the first stage. The number of enumeration areas selected within each district is proportional to the size of the district and is provided in Table 4.1 below.

The number of households selected within district x, denoted by n_{D_x} is proportional to the size of the district and was determined using the following formula:

$$n_{D_x} = \frac{N_{D_X}}{N} \cdot 400$$

where n_{D_x} represents sample size (number of households in sample) for district x where x= 1,…, 9.

N_{D_X} represents the population size (number of households in population) for district x

Table 4.1. Number of Enumeration Areas per District

District	*Number of Enumeration Areas*
Port Louis	3
Pamplemousses	3
Rivière du Rempart	3
Flacq	3
Grand Port	3
Savanne	2
Plaines Wilhems	9
Moka	2
Rivière Noire	2
Total	*30*

Source: Authors' Computation

$$N = \sum_{x=1}^{9} N_{D_x}$$

The number of households selected within each enumeration area was spread evenly across all selected enumeration areas within each district. In some rare cases, the number of households to be interviewed was larger than the number of households listed in the enumeration area. The excess number of household units was then allocated to another enumeration area within the same district. The number of households interviewed within each enumeration area is provided in Table 4.2 below.

Table 4.2. Sample Size per Enumeration Areas

Enumeration Areas	*District*	*Random Start*	*Systematic Interval*	*Sample Size*
111270	1	73	9	14
111316	1	4	3	13
111236	1	37	6	13
120110	2	202	16	15
120610	2	45	8	15
121832	2	80	7	15
130108	3	19	14	12
131802	3	46	4	12
130702	3	21	14	12
140202	4	64	7	15
141707	4	102	8	15
140641	4	94	7	15
151831	5	166	14	12
152224	5	31	14	12
150805	5	72	7	13
161212	6	8	1	8
160603	6	34	7	15
171421	7	58	5	13
171429	7	7	2	13
173336	7	15	10	15
170304	7	211	20	13

Table 4.2. (Continued)

Enumeration Areas	*District*	*Random Start*	*Systematic Interval*	*Sample Size*
172359	7	104	16	13
171168	7	57	6	13
173407	7	45	4	15
172254	7	159	16	13
180307	8	47	7	14
180704	8	76	13	13
190706	9	2	1	3
190149	9	8	3	23

Source: Authors' Computation

Each building unit within each selected enumeration area was identified and numbered in the enumeration map developed by Statistics Mauritius. A sample of households was selected then within each enumeration area using the kth systematic sampling method with a random start. The sampling interval as well as the random start drawn within each enumeration area is produced in Table 4.2. Initially, all buildings listed in the enumeration area were assumed to correspond to a household unit and the interviewers were required to skip all units that did not contain a household using the same systematic interval.

Sample Distribution – By Region

The survey was undertaken in different parts of the island to have a good coverage of Mauritians who are currently indebted. Around 28 per cent of the sample is in Plaines Wilhems (Centre and main location of towns) while 16 per cent come from Grand Port (South of the Island). Similarly we find the same percentage (around 13 per cent) in Pamplemousses (Northern Part of the island) and Savanne (Southern part of the island). This is shown in Figure 4.1 below.

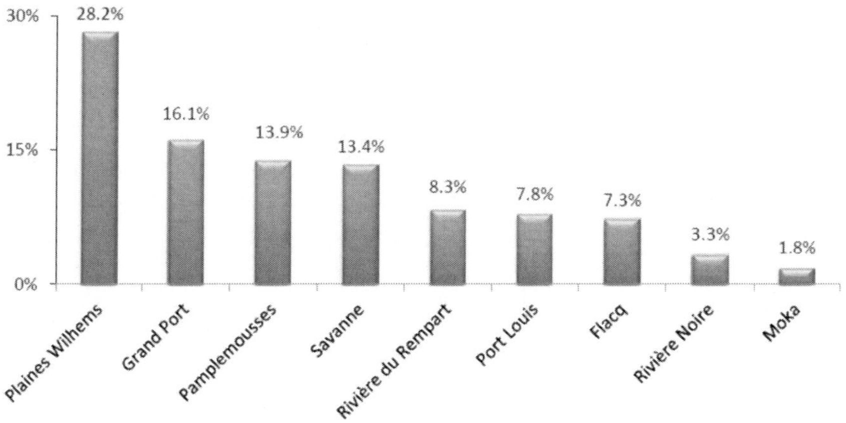

Source: Survey Data, 2014

Figure 4.1. Sample Distribution across Mauritius.

DESCRIPTIVE STATISTICS

We first analyze the socio-demographic characteristics of respondents in the sample. The characterization of indebtedness is based on variables at the household level as well as those variables at the individual level such as sex, age, marital status, education and occupational levels of the heads of household. In addition, emphasis is also laid on the household budget characteristics in terms of household income earned, assets owned, expenditure as well as the number of people working in the family. A comparison is also made with the Household Budget Survey 2012, carried out by the local statistical office (Statistics Mauritius) over 6,720 households comprising some 23,800 members. Data on the characteristics of the households such as the size and composition, the characteristics of dwellings as well as the availability of household durable goods are gathered by Statistics Mauritius.

INDIVIDUAL CHARACTERISTICS OF THE HEAD OF HOUSEHOLD

Our sample consists of 80.5 per cent of male respondents. Whilst, age was categorized into five groups, it was noted that a higher percentage of respondents (30.5 per cent) fall within the age bracket of 50-59 years whereas 27 per cent are aged between 40 and 49 years and around 22 per cent are between 30 and 39 years. This is shown in Figure 4.2 below.

In addition, we note that 86 per cent of the respondents are married, 5.6 per cent are widowed, 3.3 per cent are single and 2.8 per cent are separated (see Figure 4.3 below). Respondents provided information on their family size and around 42 per cent have 4 members in their family, 24 per cent have a family size of 3 whereas 15 and 12 per cent have 2 and 5 family members, respectively in their household. The average family size is 3.6; close to the figure of 3.5 as per the Household Budget Survey (2012) (Statistics Mauritius, 2012). From our survey, it is further observed that around 37 per cent of respondents have 2 dependent children while 32.5 per cent have only one dependent child and 8 per cent have 3 dependent children.

The education feature of the household is shown in Figure 4.4 below. A high percentage of head of households (45 per cent) have completed their School Certificate at secondary level (Form 5 educational level). Similarly, around 17 per cent have a vocational qualification in the form of a Diploma, 13 per cent have a postgraduate qualification and 7 per cent have completed pre-primary education.

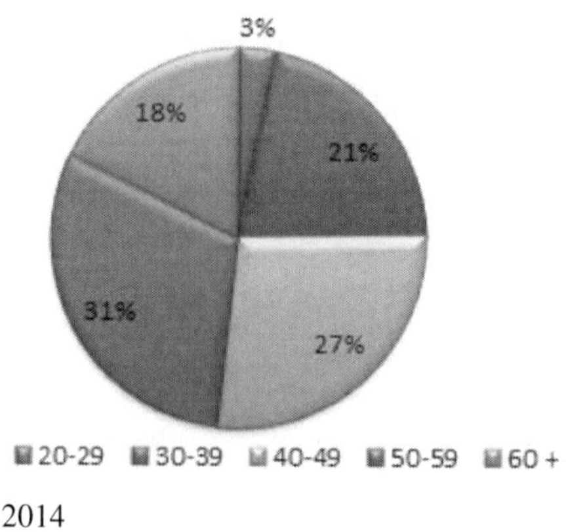

Source: Survey Data, 2014

Figure 4.2. Age Categories of Heads of Household.

In terms of occupation, 69 per cent of the sample are employees while 15 per cent have their own business, 11 per cent are unemployed and 3 per cent are retired. This is shown in Figure 4.5 below. It is further perceived that out of those respondents who are presently employees, 37 per cent work in the public sector, 57 per cent operate in the private sector and the rest (6 per cent) work in semipublic organizations.

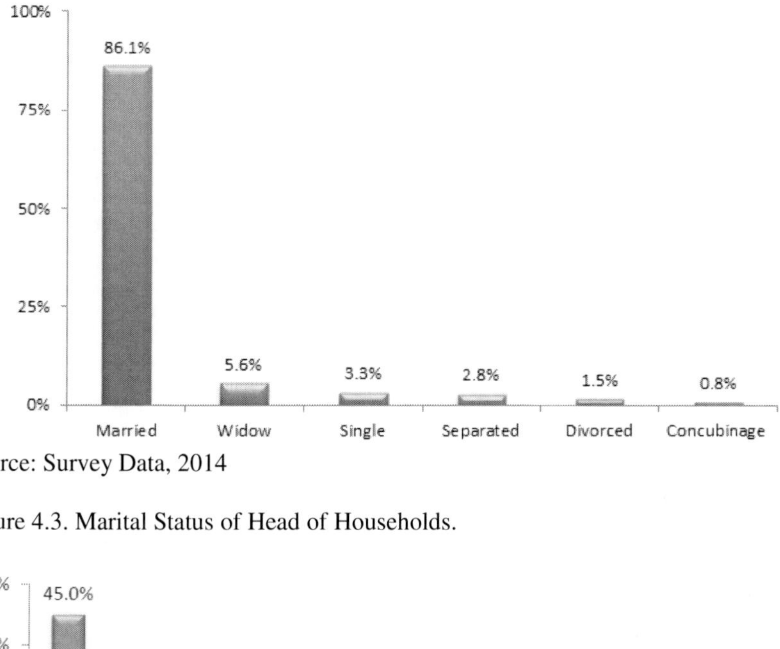

Source: Survey Data, 2014

Figure 4.3. Marital Status of Head of Households.

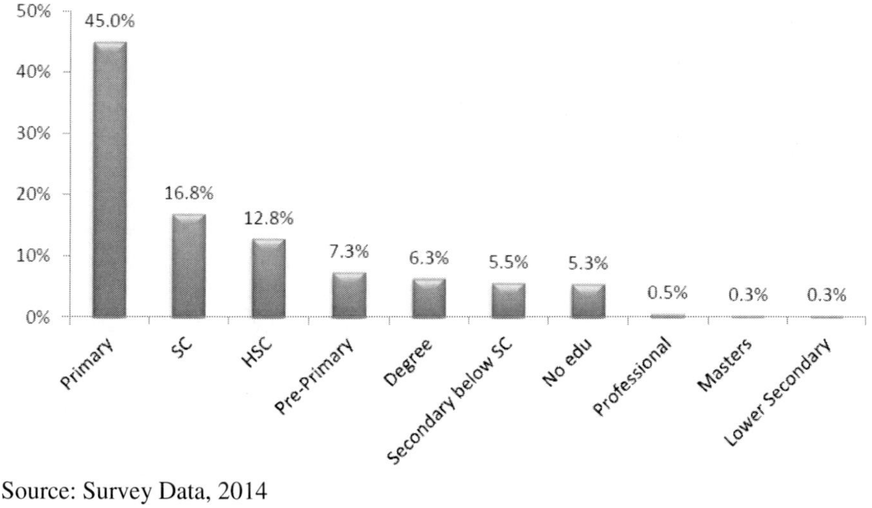

Source: Survey Data, 2014

Figure 4.4. Education Level of Heads of Household.

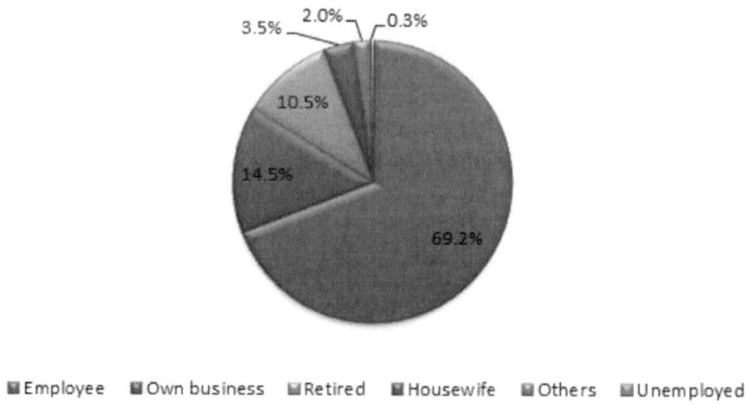

Source: Survey Data, 2014

Figure 4.5. Occupation Level of Heads of Household.

Table 4.3 below focuses on the specific sector of activity of the heads of the households in the sample. It can be seen that around 13 per cent work in administrative and support services and around the same percentage operate in agriculture, forestry and fishing. Around 10 per cent and 9 per cent are respectively working in the construction and manufacturing sectors. In addition, around 9 per cent are in wholesale and retail trade while 7 per cent are working in the transport and storage sector. Around 6 per cent work in the education sector and the same percentage can be found in arts, entertainment and recreational activities.

Table 4.3. Field of Employment of Heads of Household

Field of employment (Head)	*Frequency*	*%*
Agriculture, forestry & fishing	45	13.4
Manufacturing	31	9.2
Electricity, gas, steam & air conditioning supply	6	1.8
Water supply, sewage, waste management & remediation activities	9	2.7
Construction	34	10.1
Wholesale & retail trade; repair of motor vehicles	30	8.9
Transport & Storage	25	7.4
Accommodation & Food services	10	3.0
Information & communication	2	0.6
Financial & insurance activities	5	1.5

Field of employment (Head)	*Frequency*	*%*
Professional, scientific & technical activities	7	2.1
Administrative & support services	44	13.1
Public administration	13	3.9
Education	21	6.2
Human health & social work	18	5.3
Arts, entertainment & recreation	20	5.9
Other service activities	17	5.0
Total	*337*	*100.0*

Source: Survey Data, 2014

HOUSEHOLD BUDGET CHARACTERISTICS

The income and expenditure characteristics of the heads of household are also analysed in this section. From Figure 4.6 below, it can be seen that 22 per cent of households earn between Rs 15,001- 20,000, 21 per cent are in the income bracket of Rs 10,001-15,000, 15 per cent earn between Rs 7,501 – Rs 10,000 and 14 per cent are in the income range of Rs 20,001 – Rs 25,000. Heads of household earning between Rs 30,000 to Rs 40,000 represent 7 per cent of the sample while 4 per cent earn more than Rs 40, 000.

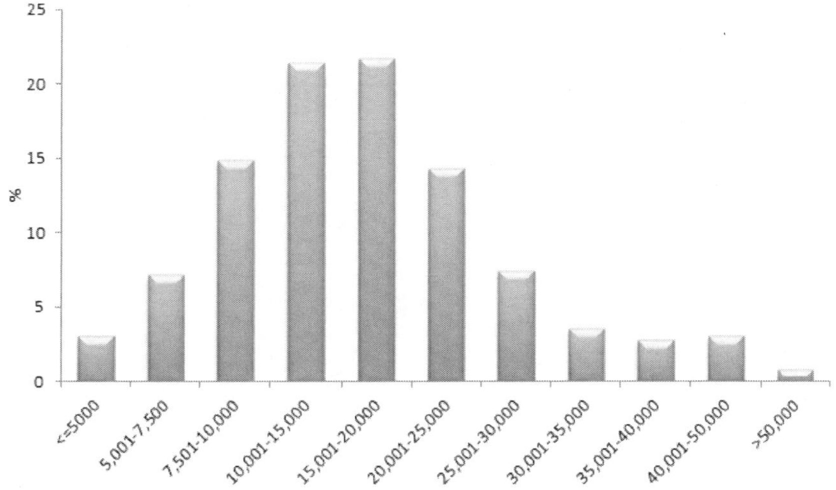

Source: Survey Data, 2014

Figure 4.6. Income Level of Heads of Household.

To ensure that the sample is representative of the population of Mauritius, the income characteristics of the survey respondents are compared with those of the latest Household Budget Survey (HBS) 2012; involving around 6,500 households. Household income is measured as the monthly total revenue received by the household including monthly salary from main job, income earned from a secondary job, income earned by wife/partner/working children and pension received by any member living under the same roof and contributing financially to the household. The same income range has been adopted as per the HBS 2012 and it is noted that our sample captures almost the same percentage of households in the different income brackets (Table 4.4 below).

Considering the gender dimension, it is further observed that a higher percentage of female-headed households falls in the lowest income groups compared to their male counterparts. 5.1 per cent of female heads receive a household income of less than Rs 5,000[1] relative to 4.7 per cent for male heads, implying that they live in absolute poverty. In fact, the probability of being poor is higher across female-headed household and feminization of poverty is a reality in Mauritius (Tandrayen-Ragoobur and Kasseeah, 2012).

Table 4.4. Total Household Income of Survey Respondents

			Gender	
Income Range	*HBS 2012*[2]	*Survey 2014*	*Male Head*	*Female Head*
<5000	3.50	4.75	4.66	5.12
5000 - <10000	10.90	12.50	11.48	16.65
10000 - <16000	18.10	27.00	26.68	28.18
16000 - <20000	11.90	13.75	13.95	12.80
20000 - <25000	13.40	16.25	15.82	17.94
25000 - <30000	9.60	10.75	10.24	12.81
30000 - <40000	12.10	9.00	10.55	2.56
40000 - <50000	7.20	2.50	2.79	1.28
>=50000	13.30	3.50	3.72	2.56

Source: Survey Data, 2014 and HBS, 2012

[1] Rs 5,000 is the very minimum level of income. Below this threshold level, households are viewed as being in absolute poverty.

[2] The HBS 2012 accounts for total household income while the third column in Table 3.4 analyses the income of the head of household.

We further illustrate the income of the head of household by the following density plot in Figure 4.7 below. The density plot of income level of household depicts a positively skewed distribution. It is clear that a high proportion of our sample relates to head of household with monthly income less than Rs 30000. Besides, the modal income of head of household is around Rs 18000 per month.

As for expenditure, the highest average expenditure component out of the household budget covers 'Food and non-alcoholic beverages', amounting to Rs 6,314, followed by transport and fuel which sums to around Rs 2,144 (see Table 4.5 below). Rent, education and insurance also comprise major elements within the household monthly expenditure. These results are comparable to those of the HBS 2012, where the largest broad category of household expenditure remains 'Food and non-alcoholic beverages' accounting for 27.3 per cent of total household consumption expenditure (Rs 6,540 per month). Next is 'Transport' with an average expenditure amounting to Rs 3,630 (Statistics Mauritius, 2012).

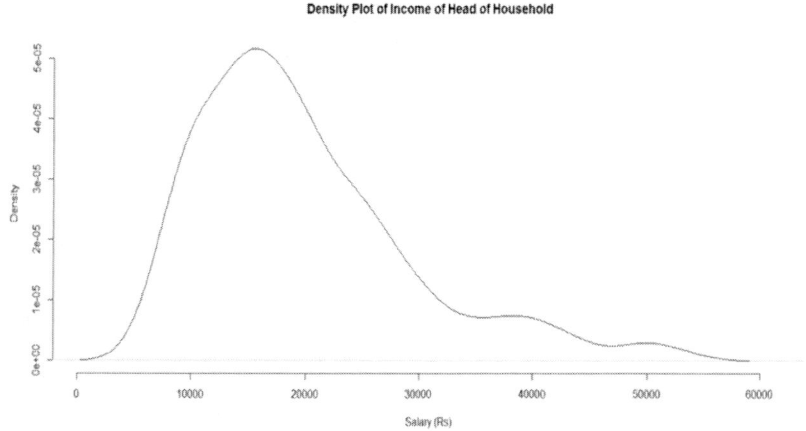

Source: Survey Data, 2014

Figure 4.7. Density Plot of Income Level of Heads of Household.

Table 4.5. Expenses of the Household

Expenses Item	*N*	*Min*	*Max*	*Mean*	*Std. Deviation*
Food & non-alcoholic drinks	400	500	15,000	6,314.0	2,779.9
Electricity	399	80	5,000	795.5	541.3
CWA & Waste water	398	15	1,000	240.0	175.1
Clothing & Footwear	253	100	9,000	653.5	751.3
Gas	397	200	3,300	485.3	245.2
Home maintenance, gardener/maid salary	115	0	12,000	564.4	1,214.5
Health	220	0	10,000	716.1	886.2
Transport & Fuel	348	100	10,000	2,143.8	1,874.0
Internet	177	0	1,500	893.3	211.4
Hobbies (Movies, pub, etc.)	115	0	3,000	600.0	492.9
Education & Tuition fees (Uniform, exam fees, stationery)	239	0	20,000	1,720.1	2,233.7
Restaurants & Hotels	156	0	3,000	666.5	537.9
Betting (Loto, horse racing, etc.)	237	40	10,000	439.5	806.8
Insurance	72	100	7,000	1,011.3	1,043.3
Private TV (canal + etc.)	125	0	8,000	947.4	709.0
Telephone & Mobile	376	50	7,000	453.9	549.3
Municipal tax	88	100	5,000	513.6	748.6
Rent	21	0	5,500	1,914.3	1,460.9
Cigarette	149	0	6,000	838.0	727.0
Alcohol	221	100	2,000	779.2	399.7
Other Expenses	6	500	5,000	2,350.0	1,770.6

Source: Survey Data, 2014

Next, we analyze whether another member of the family contributes to the household by working. It can be said that around 50 per cent of the respondents have another family member working while around 37 per cent are the sole bread winner. This is again in line with the HBS 2012, where the average number of income earners per household after adjusting for household size increased between 2006/07 and 2012. In 2012, there were 2.0 income earners for an average household size of 3.5 compared to 1.9 income earners in 2006/07 for a household size of 3.7 (Statistics Mauritius, 2012). In addition, 9 per cent have 2 more family members working while for 4 per cent, no one is presently working. These are mainly heads of households who have retired and who rely on prior savings (if any) and their monthly pension for their living (see Table 4.6 below).

Table 4.6. Number of People Working in the Family

Number of people working	*Frequency*	*%*	*Cumulative %*
0	14	3.6	3.6
1	143	36.8	40.4
2	193	49.6	90.0
3	35	9.0	99.0
4	3	0.8	99.7
5	1	0.3	100.0
Total	*389*	*100.0*	

Source: Survey Data, 2014

ASSETS OF THE HOUSEHOLDS

Indebtedness is based on variables such as the value of real assets, which is given by the sum of the value of real estate, motor vehicles and other valuables (Costa and Farinha, 2012). In the survey, we note that 89 per cent of heads of household own their house while 7.5 per cent were actually renting and 2.4 per cent were living with other family members (Table 4.7 below).

We further probe into the asset ownership of the household by examining the type and number of vehicles owned by the head of household and noted that 37 per cent of the sample own a car. Out of this percentage, 91 per cent have 1 car while around 8 per cent own 2 cars. Around 8 per cent of households own a van while around 29 per cent have a motorcycle. Among them, 6 per cent have got 2 motorcycles and 93 per cent have only one.

Table 4.7. House Ownership of Heads of Household

House	*Frequency*	*Percent*	*Valid Percent*	*Cumulative Percent*
Owner	332	83.0	89.0	89.0
Rent	28	7.0	7.5	96.5
Shared Accommodation	9	2.3	2.4	98.9
Other	4	1.0	1.1	100.0
Total	373	93.3	100.0	
Missing	27	6.8		
Total	400	100.0		

Source: Survey Data, 2014

Table 4.8. Vehicle Ownership of Heads of Household

Type of Vehicle	*Number*	*Percentage*
Car	148	37.00
1	135	91.22
2	12	8.11
3	1	0.68
Van	31	7.75
Double Cab	17	4.25
Lorry	2	0.5
Motorcycle	117	29.25
1	110	93.22
2	7	5.93
Minibus	2	0.5

Source: Survey Data, 2014

Around 16 per cent of respondents own more than 1 property or land, 3.5 per cent have more than 1 house and 98.3 per cent have more than 1 plot of land.

Chapter 5

AN ASSESSMENT OF THE FINANCIAL VULNERABILITY OF INDEBTED HOUSEHOLDS

Verena Tandrayen-Ragoobur

HOW COMMON IS HOUSEHOLD DEBT?

The process of wealth accumulation has changed over time. The past 15 years have been characterized by falling interest rates, rising housing prices, variations in the performance of financial markets, deregulation, technology and changes in economic conditions (Uppal and LaRochelle-Côté, 2015). Following these changes, both assets and debts have taken on increasing importance in family finances. Access to debts has been made easier, where in many instances little or no financial security is required to access funds.

The most basic indicator of debt problems in the literature is the amount of debt a borrower holds. Respondents were asked as to whether they have contracted any type of debt and from the survey; it is noted that 83 per cent of interviewed households have at least one type of debt while only 17 per cent do not have any type of debt. Studies for developed countries have shown similar result namely for Canada, 62 per cent of households had some form of debt in 2006 (Faruqui, 2008) and in US; roughly 74 per cent of households hold some form of debt (Barnes and Young, 2003). Daniels (2001) shows that consumer indebtedness covers 73 per cent of South African households in the urban region.

Probing further into the debt issue, the amount of debt which the head of household possesses is next analyzed. It is observed that around 15 per cent of the sample have debt amounting between Rs 100,000- Rs 200,000, 13 per cent have between Rs 15,001 to Rs 25,000 of debt while 12.5 per cent hold around Rs 55,001 to Rs 100,000 amount of debt (see Figure 5.1). We also perceive a high percentage of respondents (8.6 per cent) having debt in the range of Rs 750,001 to Rs 1,000,000 whilst around 7.4 per cent have between Rs 400,001 to Rs 500,000 of debt.

SOURCES OF INDEBTEDNESS

The source of indebtedness is next examined and the highest percentage of households (39.3 per cent) tend to have loans with banking institutions, followed by around 26 per cent being engaged in hire purchase (see Figure 5.2). In fact, as from 2001, consumption expenditure has been rising, especially with the Hire Purchase and Credit Sales Act being amended in Mauritius in 2000. The Hire Purchase Act provides for two types of credit sale agreements: The 'Credit Sale Agreement' and 'Hire Purchase Agreement'.

Under the Credit Sale Agreement, the buyer may make a payment of 50 per cent of the product and pays the balance in 12 monthly installments. In addition, the customer becomes the owner of the product once the deposit is made. Under the Hire Purchase Agreement, the customer can make a deposit according to his ability, no initial deposit is even allowed. The maximum repayment period is 30 months. The interest rate in both cases is 19 per cent, calculated as per the system of Annual Percentage Rate or on the remaining balance. It should be noted that the Hire Purchase Act provides, in case of delay in monthly payments, a penalty of 8 per cent of the amount due. Ignorance of this provision may result in the buyer's debt spiral. Further, there are still shop owners who succeed in cleverly over-charging the customer by altering the repayment conditions.

Hire purchase is in fact a business activity, which remains only partially regulated and the ideal situation would be to ensure that all small and medium-sized retail outlets comply with the provisions of the Hire Purchase and Credit Sale Act 2000 (NESC Report, 2011). The prevalence of high inflation rates eroded the purchasing power of households and curtailed slightly real consumption growth. As part of efforts by government to reform the income tax regime, the effective rate of income tax was reduced to 15 per cent as from July 2007. Tighter credit conditions resulting from the hike in interest rates coupled with high inflation; however, do not seem to have hurt consumption growth. In recent years, without a legal framework for this type of credit sales, the 'pyramid' selling has gained momentum.

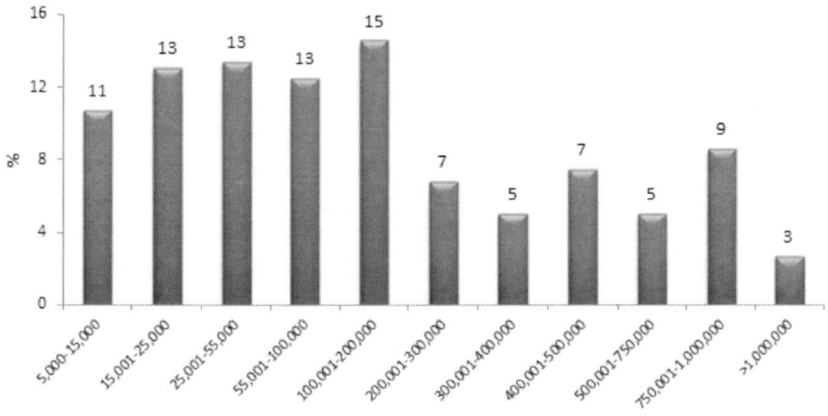

Source: Survey Data, 2014

Figure 5.1. Total Debt of the Head of Household based on Income Range.

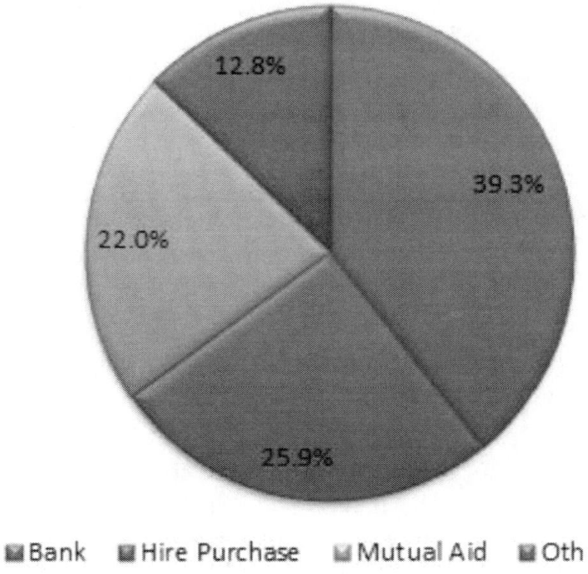

Source: Survey Data, 2014

Figure 5.2. Sources of Debt of the Head of Household.

Purpose of Debt

From Figure 5.3, it is observed that 34.4 per cent of respondents have acquired a loan for housing purposes, 25 per cent have contracted debts for the purchase of durable goods, 14 per cent for the purchase of a vehicle and 7.5 per cent for wedding expenses. Here, housing becomes a significant contributor to debt. In fact, a key feature is that debt is strongly associated with home-ownership as many home-owners have an asset — their home — more valuable than their debts. This cushion can help them to weather financial shocks (May et al., 2004).

In every country, the bulk of the increase in household debt has been in the form of borrowing for housing. For example, such borrowing currently accounts for around 75 per cent of total household debt in the United States and the United Kingdom and around 60 per cent in France and Germany, while in Australia it accounts for 85 per cent (Debelle, 2004). Mortgages have also been by far the largest component of household debt for most of the markets in Asia, ranging in share from 50 per cent to more than 80 per cent. Mortgage debt has been dominant in part because collateralized lending tends to improve the problems of adverse selection and moral hazard, and in part because many governments have promoted housing ownership (Remolona and Shim, 2008). In Mauritius, demand for housing loans has been declining in the recent years because of rising construction costs and overvaluation of property prices (Bank of Mauritius, 2014). Concurrently, consumption loans grew by 19.3 per cent as at end-March 2014 compared with growth of 17.2 per cent last year.

As regards to debt contracted for the purpose of the purchase of vehicles, a similar picture is noted in other countries where the remainder of the household debt category is consumer debt, which in the Asian region, for instance, consists mainly of loans for motor vehicles, credit card debt and education and personal loans. In Indonesia and the Philippines, motor vehicle loans have constituted a greater share of consumer debt than elsewhere in Asia and the Pacific (Remolona and Shim, 2008).

We further analyze the number of loans that a particular household has, and it is observed that 63 per cent have only one loan, while 16 per cent have 2 loans (see Figure 5.4 below). In fact most heads of household have a housing loan as well as a loan for the purchase of vehicle.

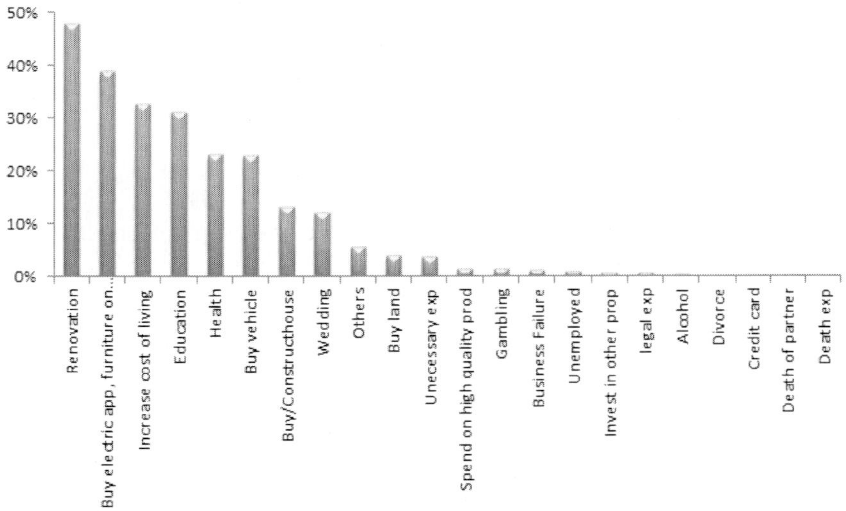

Source: Survey Data, 2014

Figure 5.3. Purpose of Debt of the Head of Household.

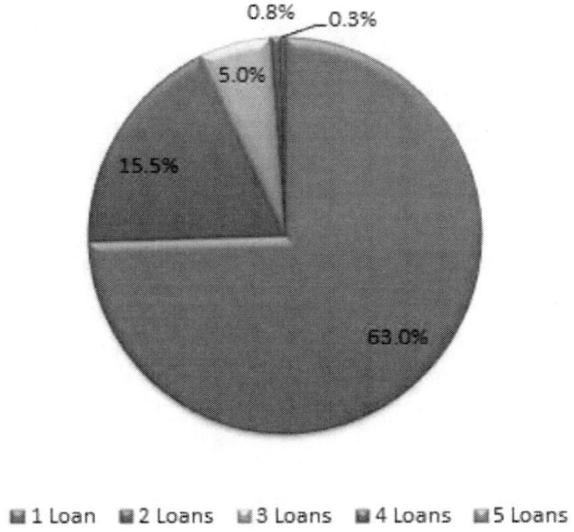

Source: Survey Data, 2014

Figure 5.4. Number of Loans of the Household.

CHARACTERISTICS OF FAMILIES WITH DEBTS

As far as indebtedness by gender is concerned, Table 5.1 indicates that there is a distinct gender dimension to indebtedness, where male-headed households (84.5 per cent) are more indebted than female-headed households (74.4 per cent). Similar results have been noted by Daniels (2001) for South Africa where male headed households were at least twice as indebted as their female counterparts.

Across marital status, married heads of household and those living with a partner are more likely to have debts. Similarly, a high percentage of divorced heads of household (80 per cent) are found to be indebted. With respect to family size, it can be seen that as the number of family members increases within the household, the higher is the probability of having debt. A larger family size implies more expenses and the need for more revenue. Larger families tend to have different characteristics compared to smaller families (Swales and Willitts, 2003). They are more likely to be out of work, and receiving social security benefits. Overall, a higher proportion of larger families than smaller families experience hardship. It is, therefore, perhaps unsurprising to observe that larger families are more likely to be indebted (Kempson, McKay and Willitts, 2004). In addition, families with 3-4 children are more likely to be indebted. This reflects the fact that having a higher number of dependent children means greater hardship for households' heads.

Moreover, heads of household with higher level of education are more likely to be indebted. This is shown by different categories of education level whereby 74 per cent of heads of household with no education have debts, while around 76 per cent of those with primary education and 80 per cent of those who have completed secondary education have debts. As we move to those households having completed tertiary education, all of them are found to be indebted. In fact, households who are better educated generally have steeper life-cycle income paths and therefore are committed to more borrowing at young ages. The increase in average educational attainment of the population is expected to push up debt accumulation (Dynan and Kohn, 2007). Tudela and Young (2005) also establish similar results for the UK.

In terms of occupation, we see that around 92 per cent of employees and 72 per cent of those having their own business are indebted. Butrica and Karamcheva (2013) show that the probability of having debt and the total value of debt are positively and significantly correlated with an individuals' propensity to work for the US. We find that employees are more likely to be indebted in Mauritius.

Table 5.1. Characteristics of Families with and without Debts

	Households with Debt	*Household With No Debts*	*% of Households with Debts*
	Number	*Number*	*Percentage*
All	326	69	82.7
Sex			
Male	268	49	84.5
Female	58	20	74.4
Age			
20-29	13	0	100.0
30-39	77	9	89.5
40-49	90	17	84.1
50-59	103	19	84.4
60+	46	24	65.7
Marital Status			
Married	289	51	85.0
Not married	37	17	69.0
Family Size			
<2	6	4	60.0
2-4	263	57	77.6
>4	59	8	88.2
Dependent Children			
0	57	20	74.0
1	100	17	85.5
2	110	22	83.3
>=3	29	3	90.6
Education			
No Education	15	6	71.4
Primary Education	22	7	75.9
Secondary Education	163	38	81.1
Diploma	58	8	87.9
Degree (Undergraduate and Postgraduate)	47	4	92.2
Professional and other qualifications	24	4	85.7
Occupation			
Employee	253	21	92.3
Own Business	42	16	72.4
Student	0	1	0.0
Unemployed	23	19	54.8
Retired	9	5	64.3
Housewife	2	6	25.0

Source: Survey Data, 2014

With respect to age, Figure 5.5 below portrays the age-debt relationship which follows an inverted-U shape relationship for the different age categories between 20 to 59 years and then the age-debt nexus rises for those beyond 60 years. Consistent with the life-cycle hypothesis, indebtedness peaks in the working age range and then gradually declines with age. This means that it is more likely that younger households, particularly those entering the housing market for the first time or raising a family, will be in debt, whereas older households, who will be building up savings for — or be enjoying — retirement, will not. Such results are expected since younger families are in the early stages of their life cycle, and thus have higher levels of debt in connection with assets held. In addition, cross sectional data from Australia, Sweden and the United States show a hump shaped pattern of debt relative to age. In aggregate, young households carry comparatively little debt relative to income (although young households who have debt, have very high levels of debt relative to income). This hump-shaped pattern follows that of home ownership, reflecting the fact that housing debt accounts for the bulk of household debt (Butrica and Karamcheva, 2013).

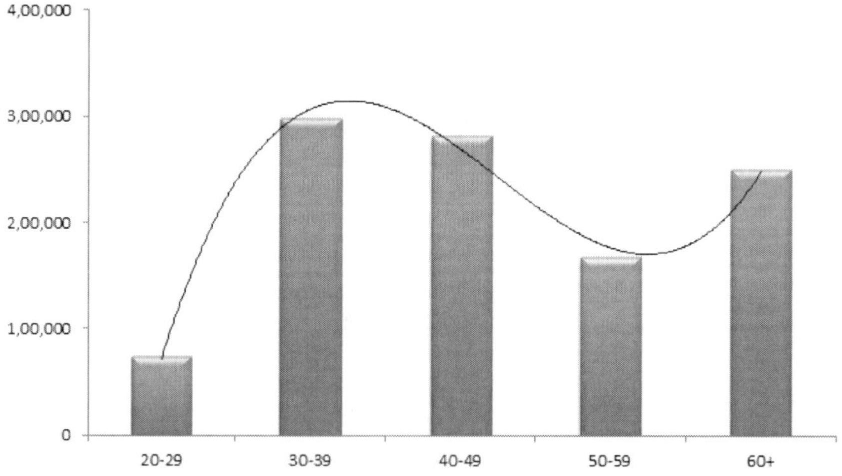

Source: Survey Data, 2014

Figure 5.5. Linking Age of Heads of Household and Average Debts.

However, for the Mauritian case, debt levels peak for individuals who are in their thirties and then decline but then rise again for those individuals being 60 and above. A high percentage of retired heads of households tends to be indebted. In fact, around 64 per cent of retired individuals have some form of debt. We postulate a N-shaped relationship between debt and age for the small island economy. This is consistent with a previous study for Germany where grandparents have large debts (Persson, 2008). Similar evidence for the US by Lusardi and Mitchell (2013) shows that even older adults on the verge of retirement (aged 56 to 61) have become increasingly more indebted. Butrica and Karamcheva (2013) further reveal that the prevalence as well as the absolute and relative value of debt among adults of retirement age (aged 62 to 69) have been increasing and even more dramatically than for those adults on the verge of retirement.

Over–Indebtedness of Mauritian Households

The Association for the Protection of Abused Borrowers (APEA) in Mauritius, a Non-Governmental Organization (NGO) postulates that 75 per cent of households are struggling to fulfill their monthly dues and 10 per cent of the households who borrowed; live in situations of over-indebtedness and can no longer pay the credits that accumulated in 2013 (Indian Ocean Times, 2013). Thus, three Mauritian households in four have difficulties to honor their debts and repay their credit. The NGO further states that 50 per cent of Mauritian households contract credits for consumption or for the acquisition of real property (Indian Ocean Times, 2013).

Hence, to measure consumer over-indebtedness, it is possible to conceptualize three broad models (Ferreira 2000; Finlay 2006; Betti et al., 2007; and Russell, Maitre and Donnelly, 2011).

The first one is an objective framework which is based on the concept of unsustainable expenditure behavior (consumption/income ratio) or unmanageable level of debt (debt/asset ratio) or inability to service the debt (debt payment/income ratio). However, there is no established critical level of these ratios beyond which a household is viewed to be over indebted (Russell, Maitre and Donnelly, 2011). According to the UK Taskforce on over-indebtedness, households are considered to be over indebted where credit commitments (excluding mortgages) exceed 25 per cent of gross income. However, Betti et al. (2007) assert that, even if a critical level of indebtedness can be established, it is likely to fluctuate widely through the life cycle of an individual.

The second model is subjective as it categorizes individuals who judge themselves unable to repay their debts unless there is a reduction in other types of expenditure. This implies that over-indebted households are those that expressed 'difficulty' or 'serious difficulty' in making debt payments, including credit debt, mortgage payments and hire purchase installments.

The third alternative records as over indebted all those cases of non-payment of debt that have been officially registered or declared before a court.

The measures of over-indebtedness used in this study combine both the objective and subjective models and are as follows:

a) High debt to income ratio
b) Arrears on utility bills
c) Proportion of households whose credit cards have been seized by the bank
d) The extent of difficulty faced by households in making monthly payments.

HIGH DEBT TO INCOME RATIO

As per Table 5.2, we first calculate total debt as a ratio of income of the head of household and analyze the difference across male and female headed households. Total debt as a share of total household income (last column) is then computed to capture over-indebtedness of the household. In Mauritius, commercial banks normally set a threshold of debt servicing at a ratio of 40 per cent of household income. In this study, we establish a range between 20 to 40 per cent to capture the percentage of over-indebted households in the sample.

From a gender perspective, male-headed households appear to be more over-indebted than their female counterparts. At 40 per cent, 5.5 per cent of households are over indebted. This same figure rises with lower threshold levels. Similar results have been noted by Gathergood (2012) where 10 per cent of UK households are over-indebted.

Table 5.2. Debt to Income Ratio

Thresholds	*Total Debt to Income Ratio (Head of Household Income) (%)*	*Male Headed (%)*	*Female Headed (%)*	*Total Debt to Income Ratio (Total Household Income) (%)*
20% and above	18.8	15.2	3.6	17.0
25% and above	15.2	12.5	2.7	14.3
30% and above	11.2	9.4	1.8	10.6
35% and above	9.1	7.6	1.5	7.9
40% and above	6.7	5.5	1.2	5.5

Source: Survey Data, 2014

Arrears on Utility Bills

High debt-to-income ratios may be taken as indicative of over-indebtedness, but it is also true that households expecting high future income growth may optimally hold high levels of debt relative to their income (Gathergood, 2012). Hence, this measure may be misleading by overstating current levels of over-indebtedness. Thus, we focus on indicators of over-indebtedness which measure delinquency on debt. In this section, the indicators of delinquency-based measures of over-indebtedness used are as follows:

- The existence of arrears on utility bills
- Proportion of households whose credit cards have been seized by the bank
- Number of months of non-payment of utility bills

In doing so, we identify how many households are currently over-indebted, that is, they have 'over-borrowed'. From the survey, it is estimated that 12.5 per cent of households have outstanding payments on their credit cards and around 3 per cent had their cards being taken back by the banks. By income quartiles, it is observed that the percentage of households re-scheduling their loans and re-cashing their loans increase as we move to higher income quartiles (see Table 5.3 (a) below).

Table 5.3 (b) focuses on households with arrears on utility bills by income quartiles, gender, age and occupation. Around 29 per cent have arrears on their utility bills, out of which, 74 per cent are male headed households. In fact around 43 per cent of households have not been able to pay their utility bills for 1 month while 36 per cent have not been able to effect payment for 2 months and 20 per cent have 3 months utility bills overdue.

The largest percentage of over-borrowers (40.5 per cent) is found in the first income quartile that is in the lowest income bracket. Further, monthly arrears on utility bills fall at higher income quartiles. Several studies have postulated that the lower the income, the greater the risk of over-indebtedness (Berthoud and Kempson 1992; Herbert and Kempson 1995; Poppe 1999; Webley and Nyhus 2001; Stamp 2006). In particular, Stamp (2006) also found that households living on low incomes were more likely to face persistent over-indebtedness, that is, those households that were below the poverty line were twice as likely to report being in arrears on credit commitments for two running years.

In addition, the highest percentage of households having arrears on bills (32.8 per cent) is in the age bracket of 50-59 years followed by 31.9 per cent of those in the age group 40-49 years. Davydoff et al. (2008) found that the likelihood of falling into arrears peaked in households headed by someone in their thirties and was also high for those in their twenties and forties. The relationship between age and debt is, however, likely to be related both to life stage and attitudes (Russell, Maitre and Donnelly, 2011).

Table 5.3(a). Recash and Reschedule of Loans and Credit Cards Status

Income Categories	*Percentage of Respondents (Reschedule Loan)*	*Percentage of Respondents (Re-cash Loan)*	*Outstanding Payments on Credit Cards*	*Card seized by the Bank*
N	338	338	48	218
% of Households	49.4	51.8	12.5	2.8
First Quartile	18.7	17.1	_	_
Second Quartile	23.4	24.0	25.0	33.3
Third Quartile	30.5	31.4	75.0	16.7
Fourth Quartile	27.5	27.4	_	50.0

Source: Survey Data, 2014

Table 5.3 (b). Arrears on Utility Bills

Categories	*Monthly Arrears on Utility Bills*	*Categories*	*Monthly Arrears on Utility Bills*
Total Households (%)	29.1	*By Income uartiles*	
Total number of Households (N)	116	First Quartile (%)	40.5
By Gender_(%)		Second Quartile (%)	26.7
Male Headed Household	74.1	Third Quartile (%)	26.7
Female Headed Household	25.9	Fourth Quartile (%)	6.0
By Age Categories_(%)		*By Occupation_(%)*	
20-29	5.2	Employee	80.2
30-39	25.9	Own Business	11.2
40-49	31.9	Unemployed	2.6
50-59	32.8	Retired	1.7
60+	4.3	Housewife	4.3

Source: Survey Data, 2014

ASSESSING THE FINANCIAL VULNERABILITY OF HOUSEHOLDS

It can be inferred that the surveyed households find it most difficult to cover their purchase of durable goods on credit as well as their utility bills and monthly expenses on foodstuffs. This is followed by expenses on fuel and education. This implies that it is becoming more difficult for the average indebted household to cover the minimum basic needs for a decent living standard (see Table 5.4 below).

Further, to assess the household financial vulnerability, we need to delve beyond the level of the debt relative to income and focus on the capacity of households to meet their debt service obligations. A financially vulnerable household is one that is required to devote a substantial portion of its income to service its debt. It faces greater exposure to negative income and interest rate shocks, and is more likely to be delinquent in its debt payments (MacDonald and Matier, 2016). Financial vulnerability is typically measured by the debt service ratio, that is, household debt payments expressed relative to disposable income (MacDonald and Matier, 2016). Financial vulnerability of the Mauritian household is further studied when considering the household debt-income relationship.

THE HOUSEHOLD DEBT-INCOME NEXUS

The link between household income and debt levels of households is next examined. Like income and wealth, debt is not distributed evenly across households. A high level of debt can be difficult to manage for some households with few assets and little income. On the other hand, high levels of debt held by some wealthy, high income households can reflect their ability to use debt to acquire further wealth. In addition, being debt free does not necessarily indicate financial wellbeing. The debt-free status of some households may reflect their inability to borrow money because lenders assess them as not being creditworthy. Such households may fail to qualify for a credit card, let alone a home loan thereby making home ownership seemingly unattainable.

Table 5.4. Financial Difficulties Encountered by Surveyed Households to Pay Monthly Expenses

Monthly Expenses	*Not Difficult*	*Less Difficult*	*Neutral*	*Difficult*	*Very Difficult*
Utility Bills	40	134	85	131	10
Rent (house)	6	12	298	16	5
Expenses on Education (Tuition, School Materials, etc.)	21	43	175	117	17
Hire Purchase	13	29	160	143	17
Transport (fuel)	27	78	148	128	10
House Loan	10	17	244	82	6
Education Loan (University Education, SC or HSC Fees)	9	21	254	53	14
Vehicle Loan	5	14	280	39	5
Payment on Credit Card	8	10	316	12	1
Monthly Expenses on Foodstuffs	25	66	89	192	27
Expenses in Own Business	4	11	286	32	3
Other Loans	1	4	191	13	1

Source: Survey Data, 2014

AVERAGE DEBT, AVERAGE DEBT AS A SHARE OF INCOME AND DEBT REPAYMENT BY INCOME CATEGORIES

To analyze the distribution of debt, income, monthly household expenditure and monthly debt payments, the household sector is divided into nine income categories. From Table 5.5 below, families whose gross incomes were less than Rs 5,000 implying these households are living in absolute poverty; have an average total debt level amounting to Rs 18,450. The highest average total debt can be seen across those families earning more than Rs 35,000 followed by those in the income bracket of Rs 30,000 – Rs 35,000 and those earning between Rs 25,000 – Rs 30,000. Average total debt as a share of income is high for those in the income bracket exceeding Rs 35,000 and those in the income bracket of Rs 30,001 – Rs 35,000 with 27.9 per cent and 24.7 per cent, respectively. This shows a positive link between income and household debt as well as income and monthly debt repayments. High income and high indebtedness tend to go hand in hand. Similar results have been obtained by Persson (2008) for a group of European countries.

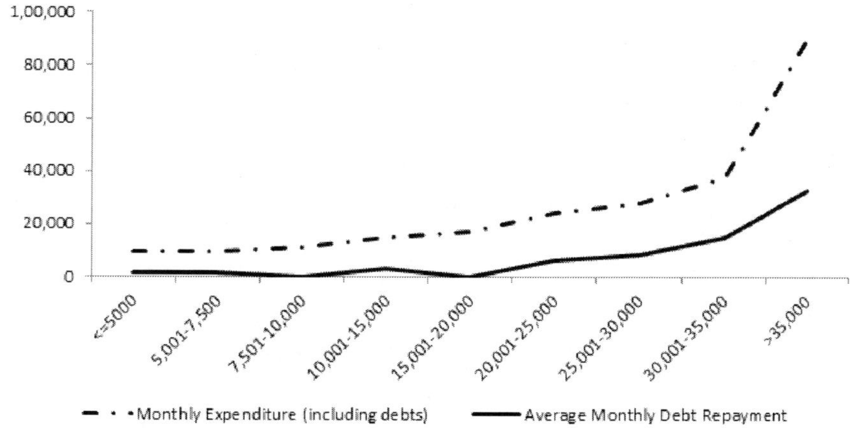

Source: Survey Data, 2014

Figure 5.6. Monthly Expenditure (including debt payments) and Monthly Debt Repayment by Income Categories.

Table 5.5. Average Debt by Income Categories of the Head of Household

Monthly Income Categories	*Monthly Expenditure (including debts)*	*Average Total Debt*	*Average Monthly Debt Repayment*	*Average Total Debt as a Share of Income*
≤ 5000	9,500	18,450	1,548	4.5
5,001-7,500	9,480.8	77,690.5	1,354.3	11.1
7,501-10,000	11,275.4	65,955.6	1,484. 7	7.3
10,001-15,000	15,157.2	133,384.1	3,023.4	10.2
15,001-20,000	17,401.4	166,200.7	4,349. 9	9.2
20,001-25,000	23,973.8	373,898	6,387.5	16.5
25,001-30,000	27,886.3	510,208.3	8,454.2	18.3
30,001-35,000	37,692.3	835,384.6	15,153.9	24.7
>35,000	90,610.0	1,243,500	32,612.2	27.9

Source: Survey Data, 2014

In particular, average monthly debt repayment tends to be very pronounced for those in the lowest income brackets. Average monthly debt repayment amounts to nearly one third of the income of those households earning on average of less or Rs 5,000 per month. This is in line with the conclusions of the Household Budget Survey carried out in 2012, whereby among indebted Mauritian households, poor ones disbursed around one-third of their income on debt repayment per month. Their analysis also shows that 1 out of every 5 households (20 per cent) in relative poverty was in debt (Statistics Mauritius, 2013). From Figure 5.6, monthly debt repayment rises with income, reaching even 50 per cent of income for those in the income bracket of Rs 30,001 to Rs 35,000.

Types of Debts by Income Quartiles

As shown in Table 5.6, irrespective of the income quartiles, households tend to incur debts essentially for housing purposes, the purchase of durable goods, followed by expenditure on vehicles and weddings. As we move to the fourth quartile, households tend to borrow money to invest in their own businesses. The number of households incurring debts to cater for durable expenditure declines as we move to the higher income quartiles, while debt incurred for the purchase of vehicles rise from the third quartile onwards. The number of households indebted for housing/land/renovation is more pronounced in the third income quartile. Wedding loan appears to be more noticeable in the second income quartile while health loan is common in the first income quartile. In fact, in the lowest quartile, households tend to be indebted mainly because of expenditure on durable goods and health services.

We can postulate the presence of demonstration effect among Mauritian consumers. From Table 5.6, it can be said that Mauritian households have similar spending behavior across the second and third income quartile. This can be seen in the types of debt incurred for durable goods, housing, and also vehicles loans. In fact, individuals' tastes and preferences are shaped by the tastes and preferences of other individuals in the economy, in the sense that upper class consumption behavior trickles down to the rest of the society, such that less rich people seek to emulate the behavior of other rich people and poor people seek to emulate the behavior of rich people (Trigg 2004). According to Veblen (1922) and Bourdieu (1979), the phenomenon of imitation exists both between and within classes such that the richest people seek further differentiation from the lower wealth categories, by consuming commodities whose price level prevents less wealthy people from consuming them.

Table 5.6. Types of Debts of the Household by Income Quartiles

	Total	*Income Quartile*			
		1	*2*	*3*	*4*
Number of Households with Debts (N)	*329*	*71*	*83*	*98*	*77*
Types of Debts					
Durable Expenditure	114	51	36	17	10
Housing/Land Loan/Renovation	160	24	31	55	50
Wedding Loan	34	8	12	9	5
Vehicle Loan	60	2	3	24	31
Health Loan (others + self)	17	6	5	5	1
Education Loan (others + self)	13	2	2	4	5
Invest in Business	25	1	2	11	11
Pay for Previous Loan	8	1	3	1	3
Non-Durable Goods	7	0	4	1	2
Others	7	0	1	3	3

Source: Survey Data, 2014

Analysis of Types of Household Debt by Income Quartiles by Median Levels

Table 5.7 shows the median amount spent by households in each quartile on different types of loans.

Across all income quartiles, housing/renovation/land loans are more pronounced. Median levels of debts (education, vehicle loan debt and other consumption loan debt) vary significantly across the household income quartiles in 2014. In fact, loans for weddings, vehicles, housing and purchase of land as well as education loans increase as we move to higher income quartiles. Debt incurred for businesses also increase for higher income quartiles, specifically in the fourth quartile.

Table 5.7. Median Levels of Types of Household Debt by Income Quartiles

Types of Debts (Median Amount, Rs)	*Income Quartile*			
	1	*2*	*3*	*4*
Durable Expenditure	17,000	25,000	30,000	75,000
Housing/Renovation/ Land Loan	302,500	400,000	290,000	700,000
Wedding Loan	80,000	100,000	200,000	300,000
Vehicle Loan	42,500	100,000	200,000	400,000
Health Loan (others + self)	30,000	55,000	427,500	100,000
Education Loan (others + self)	17,500	330,000	120,000	1,100,000
Invest in Business	200,000	58,500	100,000	700,000
Holidays	0	20,000	67,500	100,000
Pay for Previous Loan	30,000	50,000	20,000	300,000
Pay Other People Loan	0	0	80,000	0
Non-Durable Goods	0	12,500	50,000	150,000
Others	0	1,800	2,250	103,000

Source: Survey Data, 2014

CAUSES AND CONSEQUENCES OF INDEBTEDNESS

We analyze the factors explaining the rise in household debt. Home renovation works, investment in education, increased expenditure on durable goods, health problems, business failure and unemployment are among the many factors considered in increasing household borrowing. The consequences of borrowing are also assessed on the household's economic and social environment.

PERCEIVED FINANCIAL SITUATION OF HEADS OF HOUSEHOLD

In addition to the above, we assess the financial situations of heads of households in the event of debts incurred over the years. They were first interviewed on their present financial situation and it is observed that 60 per cent of households try to meet the two ends with difficulties. For 23 per cent of them, the situation is difficult to cope with. This is shown in Figure 5.7 below.

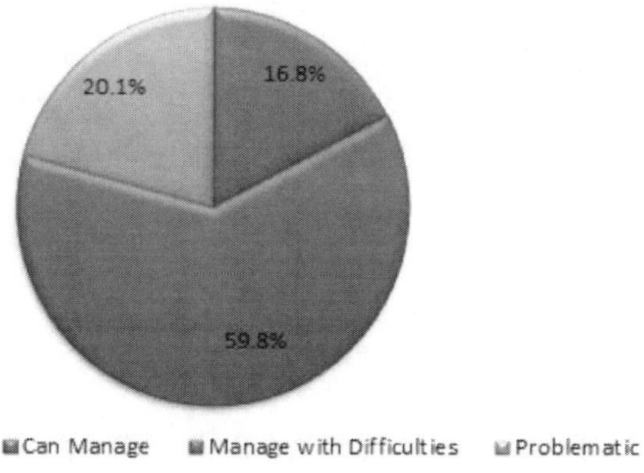

Source: Survey Data, 2014

Figure 5.7. Financial Situation of Heads of Household Surveyed.

Households believe that their financial position has worsened over the years as a result of various factors, namely, high interest rates on loans, rising cost of living, shorter period for repayment of loans and investment in properties, among others. From the survey, it is found that 82 per cent believe that the rate of interest on loans is too high, 56 per cent believe that loan repayment time is too short, 93 per cent state that the cost of living has been escalating over the years and 32 per cent have been investing in properties.

Causes of Indebtedness

The main causes of indebtedness of the Mauritian households surveyed in 2014 in terms of priority are ranked in Table 5.8. A ranking 1 implies the main cause of household indebtedness. We can infer that rising renovation works at home, hire purchase of durable goods, higher cost of living, purchase of house and purchase of vehicles are the main reasons explaining indebtedness of the Mauritian household. These are followed by wedding expenses and expenditure on education and health.

The existing evidence shows that some households may choose mortgages or other collaterized debt. Mortgages are chiefly signed for housing purchases or real estate and occasionally for purchase of big-ticket items with non-trivial resale value, such as cars (Bertola and Hochguertel, 2005). Dynan and Kohn (2007) also consider the causes and consequences of the dramatic increase in household indebtedness in the US. Their findings indicate that changes in tastes, interest rates, and households' expected incomes do not appear to have materially increased household borrowing while demographic shifts explain part of the run-up in debt. The increase in house prices particularly, but not exclusively, appears to have played the central role.

The social comparison theory can partly be used to explain the participation of Mauritian households in the debt market. Cameron and Golby (1991) have recognized the social comparison process as an important mechanism in both savings and borrowing, proposing that people save to keep up with their social reference group. Similarly, people borrow in order to acquire goods necessary to keep up with their reference group. Watson (2003) measures behavior by variables such as self-esteem, self-worth, self-image, identity and social status, and find that highly materialistic people are more likely to view themselves as spenders and to have more favorable attitudes to borrowing. The more materialistic individuals are, the more credit cards they own, the more the finance charges are on those credit cards, and the more likely they are to have loans. Livingstone and Lunt (1992) also find that those in debt considered that enjoyment requires higher consumption and therefore lower savings. Despite this, there is evidence of a negative association between materialism and happiness (Livingstone and Lunt, 1992).

CONSEQUENCES OF HOUSEHOLD INDEBTEDNESS

One major consequence of household indebtedness in the sample purports to be over stress and depression with 33.3 per cent of households stating that they are stressed with their present debt situation. This is in line with Dunn and Mirzaie (2013) where households interviewed frequently referred to depression, anxiety and stress related to their debt problems. Health problems are also encountered as a result of high debt and for 18.1 per cent of heads of household this has led to alcoholism and for 16.5 per cent of them to smoking. This is shown in Table 5.9.

Table 5.8. Main Causes of Indebtedness

Main Causes of Indebtedness	*RANKING (Number of Households) HIGHEST RANKING is 1*				
	1	2	3	4	5
Renovation Works at Home	82	53	46	11	-
Hire Purchase (Durable Goods)	61	48	38	7	2
Rising Cost of Living	44	38	31	12	7
Purchase of House	36	7	7	3	-
Purchase of Vehicles	33	40	10	8	1
Investment in Education	28	49	39	7	2
Health Problems	26	37	26	3	1
Wedding Expenses	25	14	5	3	2
Purchase of Land	8	3	2	1	2
Business Failure	3	2	-	-	-
Unemployment	1	2	-	1	-
Expenditure on High Quality Goods	1	2	1	1	1
Gambling	1	2	3	-	-
Investment in another /Secondary House	-	-	-	1	1
Alcohol Problems	-	1	-	-	1
Handicapped Member	-	1	1	1	-
Demonstration Effects	-	1	4	3	7

Source: Survey Data, 2014

Table 5.9. Consequences of Household Indebtedness

	Number of Households	*% of Households*
Stress	79	33.3
Alcoholism	43	18.1
Health problems	42	17.7
Smoking	39	16.5
Unable to work	18	7.6
Domestic violence	7	3
Family breakdown	5	2.1
Others	3	1.3
Selling of Assets for Debt Repayment	1	0.4

Source: Survey Data, 2014

Family breakdown and domestic violence are also seen as important consequences of household indebtedness. Experience of domestic violence, personal injury, clinical negligence and relationship breakdown significantly increased the likelihood of debt problems in UK (Balmer et al., 2006). However, the relationship between these factors and indebtedness can run in another direction. For instance, according to Balmer et al. (2006), relationship breakdown (and other key variables such as ill health) is a significant predictor of debt problems. Kempson et al. (2004) find that domestic violence and relationship breakdown problems more often occurred before debt problems, indicating the severe change in circumstances that can follow family breakdown. Relationship breakdown or marital separation are considered as the primary cause of debt problems in UK so much that single parents, followed by couples with children, have the highest rates of debts (Edwards, 2003).

Indebtedness of the household may lead to stress, ill-health, alcoholism, domestic violence, family breakdown, home repossession, suicide and divorce. Some households may experience utility disconnection where they no longer have access to water and electricity, among others. Ill health of the householder also leads to job losses, hence households may find it difficult to find money for essential needs, such as food or healthcare. In many cases, it can lead to poverty. Moreover, the financial strain and worry of being in debt may lead to a decline in psychological well-being, financial distress and severe psychological problems in the general population (Roberts et al., 1998).

In fact, this is in line with previous studies on the consequences of household debts on household members. At the individual level, household indebtedness has negative impact on the livelihood of households pertaining to different income categories. There is strong support in the literature for a correlation between debt burdens and both bad physical and mental health (see for instance Marmot et al., 1997; Kempson, 2002; Brown et al., 2005 and Duygan-Bump and Grant, 2009). Many of the factors, which lead to indebtedness, are outside the control of family members and affect negatively the individual, household, society and the economy. The effects of excessive borrowing by householders are wide ranging, with damaging effects on family relationships.

Chapter 6

ECONOMETRIC ANALYSIS AND FINDINGS

Verena Tandrayen-Ragoobur

ECONOMETRIC SPECIFICATIONS

When households choose to borrow, they also have to take a decision regarding the extent of indebtedness (Costa and Farinha, 2012). We characterize the households' participation in the debt market and their level of indebtedness in relation to relevant economic, social, and demographic features as specified by equations (1) and (2). There is a general consensus also that the total amount of debt is conditional on the variables used at household level. Thus, the characterization of indebtedness is based on variables such as the value of income, the ownership of assets, the household size as well as on variables at the individual level such as the age, sex, marital status, education level and work status of the individual in the household as shown below:

$$lnTotalDebt_i = \delta_0 + \delta_1 Age_i + \delta_2 Sex_i + \delta_3 FamilySize_i + \delta_4 MaritalStatus_i + \delta_5 Education_i + \delta_6 lnHouseholdIncome_i + \delta_7 HouseOwnership_i + \delta_8 CarOWnership_i + \delta_9 OtherProperties_i + \delta_{10} Sector\ of\ Activity_i + \varepsilon_i \quad (1)$$

$$lnTotalDebt_i = \delta_0 + \delta_1 Age_i + \delta_2 Sex_i + \delta_3 FamilySize_i + \delta_4 MaritalStatus_i + \delta_5 Education_i + \delta_6 IncomeQuartiles_i + \delta_7 HouseOwnership_i + \delta_8 CarOWnership_i + \delta_9 OtherProperties_i + \delta_{10} Sector\ of\ Activity_i + \varepsilon_i \quad (2)$$

where *ln* represents log of the variable and *i* represents the individual in the sample. The dependent variable *Debt* is total debt contracted by the household. *Age* denotes the age of the respondent in terms of number of years and different age categories are included as dummies. *Sex* is included as a dummy variable with the value of 1 for male and 0 for female head of household. *FamilySize* controls for the number of members within the family. *MaritalStatus* denotes whether the person is married, divorced, widowed, separated, single or lived with a partner. The variable *Education* controls for the level of education of the household namely no education, primary education, secondary education, tertiary education and professional qualifications. In addition, *HouseOwnership* captures whether the respondent owns or rents a house or lives with friends/family members. *CarOwnership* also measures the asset of the respondent and is a dummy variable being 1 if the head of household has a car and 0 otherwise while *OtherProperties* denotes whether the head of household has other properties (in which case the dummy takes a value of 1) or not (dummy being 0 in this case). The sector of activity *(SectorActivity)* is also specified to capture the sector in which the individual is working whether in the public, private or informal sector.

According to economic theory, the selection of the explanatory variables used in the regression analysis takes into account that households' decisions concerning debt are largely determined by the objective of smoothing consumption over the life-cycle (Friedman, 1957; Modigliani, 1986 and Costa and Farinha, 2012). Households take investment decisions, in particular the decision on the acquisition of the household's main residence and durable goods among others (Costa and Farinha, 2012). Household's income *(lnhouseholdIncome)* is in turn given by the sum of regular income received individually by the household (employee income, income from self-employment, income from secondary job) and income from partner or another working family member and income from pensions. Household Income is further split into 4 quartiles (refer to equation (2)) to see the difference in total debt levels and debt repayment across income levels.

To capture the debt repayment situation of the Mauritian households and the factors influencing same, the dependent variable is amended in equations (1) and (2) and is replaced by the log of the amount of total debt repayment by the household *(lnDebtRepayment)*. This is depicted by equations (3) and (4).

$$lnDebtRepayment_i = \sigma_0 + \sigma_1 Age_i + \sigma_2 Sex_i + \sigma_3 FamilySize_i + \sigma_4 MaritalStatus_i + \sigma_5 Education_i + \sigma_6 lnHouseholdIncome_i + \sigma_7$$

$HouseOwnership_i + \sigma_8\, CarOWnership_i + \sigma_9\, OtherProperties_i + \sigma_{10}\, Sector\ of\ Activity_i + \varepsilon_i$ (3)

$$lnDebtRepayment_i = \alpha_0 + \alpha_1 Age_i + \alpha_2 Sex_i + \alpha_3 FamilySize_i + \alpha_4 MaritalStatus_i + \alpha_5 Education_i + \alpha_6 IncomeQuartiles_i + \alpha_7 HouseOwnership_i + \alpha_8 CarOWnership_i + \alpha_9 OtherProperties_i + \alpha_{10} Sector\ of\ Activity_i + \varepsilon_I \quad (4)$$

The next set of equation examines over indebtedness of Mauritian households. Based on the analysis in Chapter 5, the different threshold levels of debts as a share of income are used and equation (5) estimates over indebtedness across Mauritian households as follows:

$$Overindebtedness_i = \varphi_0 + \varphi_1 Age_i + \varphi_2 Sex_i + \varphi_3 FamilySize_i + \varphi_4 MaritalStatus_i + \varphi_5 Education_i + \varphi_6 IncomeQuartiles_i + \varphi_7 HouseOwnership_i + \varphi_8 CarOWnership_i + \varphi_9 OtherProperties_i + \varphi_{10} Sector\ of\ Activity_i + \varepsilon_I \quad (5)$$

Since there is no official critical level for these ratios, we establish a range between 20 to 40 per cent to capture the percentage of over-indebted households in the sample. For equation (5), the dependent variable is a dummy variable with a value of 1 for those households above the threshold of total debt as a share of household income (that is the over indebted households) and 0 otherwise. All the other variables are as defined above.

Estimation Technique

Preliminary checks were performed to detect the presence of major outliers and to test for heteroscedasticity. This is done using the Cook and Weisberg (1983) test. We also use the Shapiro-Wilk test for normal data and the Kernel density estimates to test for the normality of the residuals. Since there is no serious problem, OLS technique is applied to the cross sectional data.

For equation (5), as the dependent variable is a dummy, logistic regression is applied. This technique is used to predict the probability of occurrence of an event by fitting data to a logistic curve. Like many forms of regression analysis, it makes use of several predictor variables that may be either numerical or categorical. Logistic regression is as an alternative technique to overcome limitations of Ordinary Least Squares (OLS) regression in handling dichotomous outcomes. The logistic function, which, like probabilities, always takes on values between zero and one:

$$f(z) = \frac{e^z}{e^z + 1} = \frac{1}{1 + e^{-z}}$$

The input is z and the output is $f(z)$. The logistic function is useful because it can take as an input any value from negative infinity to positive infinity, whereas the output is confined to values between 0 and 1. The variable z represents the exposure to some set of independent variables, while $f(z)$ represents the probability of a particular outcome, given that set of explanatory variables. The variable z is a measure of the total contribution of all the independent variables used in the model. Logistic regression uses Maximum Likelihood technique to get the estimates of the coefficients. The coefficients in the output of the logistic regression are given in units of log odds (that is logarithm of the odds). The coefficients indicate the amount of change expected in the log odds when there is a one unit change in the predictor variable with all of the other variables in the model being held constant. A positive regression coefficient means that the explanatory variable increases the probability of the outcome, while a negative regression coefficient is interpreted otherwise.

DEBT BEHAVIOR OF MAURITIAN HOUSEHOLDS

Total Debts and Debts as a Share of Income of the Household

The first part of this chapter includes the estimation results of regressions in which the dependent variables are firstly, the total debt of the household and second, total debt as a share of household income. These results identify the socio-economic and demographic characteristics of indebted households in Mauritius. Table 6.1 presents the OLS results from equations (1) and (2) where the dependent variable is total household debt. Similarly Table 6.2 depicts the results where the dependent variable is total household debt as a share of income.

From Table 6.1, the results reveal that those in the age groups of 30 to 39 and 40 to 49 tend to have higher debt levels relative to the benchmark category of households in the age bracket of 20 to 29 years. This profile is related to the fact that households in the working group, have a greater need/opportunity to apply for credit as their current income is lower than their expected future income and they have a longer life expectancy. The debt market participation of the youngest households is; however, lower than the participation of those in the second age class. In fact, the greater uncertainty concerning future income in the case of the very young households may lead to a lower demand for loans (Costa and Farinha, 2012).

Table 6.1. Regression Results of Debt Behavior of Mauritian Households (Total Household Debt as Dependent Variable)

Dependent Variable	*LnTotal Debt*			
Age 30 to 39	0.647	0.611	0.691	0.681
	(2.33)**	(2.51)**	(2.49)**	(2.54)**
Age 40 to 49	0.611	0.491	0.633	0.552
	(2.13)**	(1.95)*	(2.27)**	(2.07)**
Age 50 to 59	0.205	0.129	0.297	0.351
	(0.72)	(0.51)	(1.07)	(1.33)
Age 60+	0.602	0.471	0.994	0.386
	(1.75)*	(1.47)	(2.84)***	(1.10)
Male	-0.048	0.022	-0.049	0.013
	(0.28)	(0.14)	(0.29)	(0.07)
Family size – 4	0.347	0.406	0.302	0.669
	(2.03)**	(2.27)**	(1.87)*	(3.43)***
Family size - 5	0.712	0.846	0.733	1.253
	(3.28)***	(3.87)***	(3.29)***	(5.18)***
Married	-0.328	-0.326	-0.266	-0.450
	(1.45)	(1.47)	(1.14)	(1.90)
Primary Education	0.244	0.257	0.236	0.332
	(0.75)	(0.78)	(0.70)	(0.87)
Secondary Education	0.380	0.362	0.313	0.461
	(1.38)	(1.29)	(1.06)	(1.37)
Tertiary Education	0.544	0.516	0.493	0.798
	(1.72)*	(1.65)*	(1.51)	(2.17)**
Professional	0.762	0.734	0.798	1.084
	(1.94)*	(1.81)**	(2.01)**	(2.39)**
Ln household Income	1.215	-	-	-
	(6.81)***	-	-	-
Owner	-0.102	-0.050	-0.078	0.0003
	(0.61)	(0.30)	(0.45)	(0.00)

Table 6.1. (Continued)

Dependent Variable	*LnTotal Debt*			
Public Sector	0.299	0.309	0.332	0.343
	(1.53)	(1.65)*	(1.65)*	(1.71)*
Private Sector	-0.470	-0.477	-0.500	-0.537
	(2.76)***	(2.76)***	(2.85)***	(2.97)***
Other Properties	0.409	0.344	0.366	0.217
	(2.08)**	(1.74)*	(1.71)*	(1.03)
Car Ownership	0.633	0.577	0.584	0.717
	(3.60)***	(3.13)***	(3.29)***	(4.00)***
Ln household Income Second Quartile		0.530	-	-
	-	(2.64)***	-	-
Ln household Third Quartile	-	0.968	-	-
	-	(4.02)***	-	-
Ln household Income Fourth Quartile	-	1.929	-	-
	-	(7.24)***	-	-
Ln Monthly Salary	-	-	1.133	-
	-	-	(7.14)***	-
Ln Monthly Salary Second Quartile	-	-	-	0.353
	-	-	-	(1.65)*
Ln Monthly Salary Third Quartile	-	-	-	0.641
	-	-	-	(2.80)**
Ln Monthly Salary Fourth Quartile	-	-	-	1.252
	-	-	-	(4.63)***
Constant	-1.719	9.216	-0.842	9.088
	(1.08)	(23.93)***	(0.59)	(20.56)***
F-test	26.40	23.94	23.98	20.33
R^2	0.54	0.55	0.51	0.49
N	327	328	315	328

** $p < 0.05$; *** $p < 0.01$, *$p < 0.10$

Source: Authors' Computation

In addition, the coefficient of the age dummy for the age category 60 years and above (Age 60+) is larger compared to the age group of 50 to 59 years and relative to the youngest age category of 20 to 29 years. This implies that debt levels of retired persons seem to be on the high side in Mauritius. A finding which is very peculiar to the Mauritian context where the ageing population is increasing over the years and their retirement pensions or any other sources of income may not provide a decent living. The coefficients of the age dummies further support the N-shaped link between age and debt levels. The alarming warning contradicts the stereotype of younger people being the most indebted and highlights the financial difficulty many older people are suffering after they retire. One possible explanation for this trend, is that older people are unable to easily increase their income; meaning that any debt they have when they stop work, becomes unsustainable more quickly than those who are actually in employment.

Not surprisingly, household size is closely linked to the level of debt. Family formation is one of the key life stages captured by the life-cycle model. People have traditionally partnered and have children at the start of their working life, This therefore explains the relatively high ratio of borrowing to saving at this life stage: incomes are low and costs are high. However, increasingly in Mauritius, the trend in forming an "average" family is occurring at a later stage of life. Partnering now requires that both partners are well educated and have each a secure job. There is mixed evidence as to the effect that family size has on the use of debt or indebtedness (Legge and Heynes, 2009). Livingstone and Lunt (1992) show a negative but insignificant relationship between use of debt and number of children. The mixed results may be due to confounding factors such as age, income and wealth. In fact, the link with indebtedness may vary depending on the representativeness of survey data of the age of the family and family incomes (Legge and Heynes, 2009). In the Mauritian sample, it is observed that larger family size is directly linked with more dependent children, hereby explaining higher expenditure on medical services, education and food requirements. Households with larger family size thus seem to be more financially constrained and indebted compared to those with smaller family size. Similar results have been found by Costa and Farinha (2012) for Portugal.

Similarly, households' total debt increases with the level of education. We observe that households with tertiary education have higher levels of debts compared to the benchmark dummy that is those with no education. Tudela and Young (2005) also show that debt increases with the individual's qualifications for the UK. Further, Bridges and Disney (2004) for the UK again, postulate that the main microeconomic determinants of household debt are income, age of head of household, family size, home ownership, profession and other attitudinal factors. Households who are more educated have thus steeper life-cycle income paths and hence have relatively more borrowing at young ages. The increase in average educational attainment of the population is then expected to push up debt accumulation (Bridges and Disney, 2004). Nonetheless, higher education breeds more stable employment, higher income and better financial literacy (Legge and Heynes, 2009).

Households with members working in the public sector are more likely to have larger amount of debts relative to those who work in the quasi-public sector while those working in the private sector have lower debt levels compared to those in the quasi-public sector with a statistically significant negative coefficient. This is in line with Abid et al. (2012) who establish that the profession of the household influences the development of household indebtedness in Tunisia. Government officials may find it less risky to hold debts due to job security and other pecuniary benefits they can accede to in the public sector where as the risk levels are much higher for those working in the private sector.

Besides, high disposable income, high indebtedness and large assets tend to go hand in hand. Nevertheless, the relationship between income and borrowing is not straightforward. In theory, as income increases, the individual can afford to service more debt. However, income tend to increase with age, and the life-cycle model suggests that people's propensity or need to borrow declines as they age and accumulate wealth. Hence, the question which remains to be answered is: which effect is greater? Is income positively related to indebtedness, but negatively to over-indebtedness? From our survey, we noted that since debts increase with age, the overall effect of income on indebtedness of household is likely to be positive. Hence, the findings show that the positive relationship between income and debt levels is not only robust across total household income and its different categories but also across the head of household's income alone. Higher levels of total household debt are held by the highest income quartile. Similar findings are those of Magri (2002) for Italian households where the probability of having debt is positively influenced by age and income. It is found that the role of income is important, with the uncertainty of income reducing the demand for loans. Assets of households in terms of car ownership and ownership of other properties are positively related to the households' debt levels.

Using a variant of the dependent variable, namely total debt as a share of total income, similar regression results are obtained. Though disposable income seems to be irrelevant as to the decision of participating in the debt market, but it is a moderate predictor of how far the individual gets into debt (that is the amount of debts taken) and an important predictor of how much one repays (that is debt repayments) (Legge and Hennes, 2009). Repayments are also predicted by the amount owed: the more one owes, the more one repays, provided one has the resources to do so (Livingstone and Lunt, 1992).

Table 6.2. Regression Results of Debt Behavior of Mauritian Households (Total Debt as a Share of Income as Dependent Variable)

Dependent Variable	*lndebtincome*			
Age 30 to 39	0.675	0.711	0.691	0.726
	(2.46)*	(2.85)***	(2.49)**	(2.76)***
Age 40 to 49	0.598	0.594	0.633	0.615
	(2.15)**	(2.36)**	(2.27)**	(2.34)**
Age 50 to 59	0.213	0.230	0.297	0.317
	(0.77)	(0.90)	(1.07)	(1.20)
Age 60+	0.915	0.946	0.994	0.975
	(2.61)***	(2.91)***	(2.84)***	(2.92)***
Male	-0.067	-0.053	-0.049	-0.048
	(0.39)	(0.33)	(0.29)	(0.30)
Family Size - 4	0.251	0.273	0.302	0.318
	(1.57)	(1.66)*	(1.87)*	(1.92)
Family Size - 5	0.680	0.715	0.733	0.801
	(3.15)***	(3.28)***	(3.29)***	(3.61)***
Married	-0.289	-0.271	-0.266	-0.273
	(1.25)	(1.22)	(1.14)	(1.20)
Primary Education	0.283	0.266	0.236	0.245
	(0.85)	(0.82)	(0.70)	(0.73)
Secondary Education	0.313	0.275	0.313	0.293
	(1.08)	(0.97)	(1.06)	(1.00)
Tertiary Education	0.433	0.370	0.493	0.473
	(1.36)	(1.18)	(1.51)	(1.44)
Professional	0.643	0.513	0.798	0.663
	(1.65)*	(1.30)	(2.01)**	(1.65)*
Ln household Income	0.403	–	–	–
	(2.14)**	–	–	–
Owner	-0.117	-0.087	-0.078	-0.073
	(0.68)	(0.51)	(0.45)	(0.41)
Public Sector	0.341	0.373	0.332	0.361
	(1.71)*	(1.90)*	(1.65)*	(1.79)*
Private Sector	-0.441	-0.451	-0.500	-0.493
	(2.54)**	(2.61)***	(2.85)***	(2.85)***
Other Property	0.361	0.352	0.366	0.321
	(1.70)*	(1.67)*	(1.71)*	(1.47)
Car ownership	0.507	0.449	0.584	0.516
	(2.81)***	(2.47)**	(3.29)***	(2.88)***

Table 6.2. (Continued)

Dependent Variable	*lndebtincome*			
Ln household Income Second Quartile	_	-0.051	_	_
	_	(0.25)	_	_
Ln household Third Quartile	_	0.088	_	_
	_	(0.37)	_	_
Ln household Income Fourth Quartile	_	0.677	_	_
	_	(2.55)**	_	_
Ln Monthly Salary	_	_	0.133	_
	_	_	(0.84)	_
Ln Monthly Salary Second Quartile	_	_	_	-0.080
	_	_	_	(0.38)
Ln Monthly Salary Third Quartile	_	_	_	0.001
	_	_	_	(0.01)
Ln Monthly Salary Fourth Quartile	_	_	_	0.368
	_	_	_	(1.41)
Constant	-3.311	0.415	-0.842	0.393
	(1.91)*	(1.07)	(0.59)	(0.98)
F-test	10.75	10.71	10.30	10.00
R^2	0.34	0.36	0.33	0.33
N	314	315	315	315

* *$p < 0.05$; *** $p < 0.01$, *$p < 0.1$
Source: Authors' Computation

The debt-to-income ratio is considered to be one of the most important indicators of a family's indebtedness and actually means debt sustainability. A sharp increase in household debt to income ratio raised concerns about a parallel rise in household financial vulnerability. A high debt-to-income ratio signals that the household has too much debt for the amount of income it has, and lenders view this as a signal that the household will be unable to take on any additional debt. Families with higher debt-to-income ratios spend more of their income on debt repayments and are more likely to be financially strained. The higher debt to income ratio also implies that households will be more exposed to shocks. Our results reveal that debt to income ratio is positive and statistically significant for those families in the highest income bracket (fourth quartile). The findings remain robust across age groups, education and occupation levels and income categories amongst others. This is shown in Table 6.2.

Debt Repayments of the Households

In particular, the debt service ratio is a better metric for evaluating the burden and sustainability of household debt than the ratio of debt to income. Families with a relatively high debt-to-income ratio are more likely to spend a higher proportion of their income on repaying their debt, leaving less for other consumption (or saving). The regression results using debt repayments and debt repayments as a share of income as dependent variables on the sample of Mauritian households are thus presented in Tables 6.3 and 6.4 respectively. The OLS results for equations (3) and (4) are tabled and the evidence for total debt repayment is in line with the above results.

Table 6.3. Regression Results of Debt Behavior of Mauritian Households (Total Debt Repayment as Dependent Variable)

Dependent Variable	*lndebtrepayment*			
Age 30 to 39	0.505	0.446	0.546	0.512
	(2.62)***	(2.53)**	(2.91)***	(2.66)***
Age 40 to 49	0.555	0.445	0.574	0.486
	(2.83)***	(2.54)**	(3.19)***	(2.64)***
Age 50 to 59	0.374	0.298	0.443	0.441
	(1.88)*	(1.65)*	(2.38)**	(2.35)**
Age 60+	0.679	0.551	1.039	0.473
	(3.06)***	(2.58)**	(4.57)***	(2.01)**
Male	0.024	0.093	0.024	0.080
	(0.24)	(0.97)	(0.23)	(0.74)
Family Size - 4	0.194	0.244	0.136	0.429
	(1.58)	(1.88)*	(1.11)	(2.89)***
Family Size - 5	0.404	0.513	0.392	0.824
	(2.73)***	(3.25)***	(2.59)***	(4.59)***
Married	-0.191	-0.193	-0.131	-0.315
	(1.44)	(1.43)	(0.94)	(2.18)**
Primary Education	0.530	0.530	0.493	0.611
	(1.98)**	(1.89)*	(1.89)*	(2.01)**
Secondary Education	0.646	0.638	0.549	0.721
	(2.88)***	(2.64)***	(2.38)**	(2.57)**

Table 6.3. (Continued)

Dependent Variable	*Indebtrepayment*			
Tertiary Education	0.796	0.800	0.697	0.987
	(3.44)***	(3.25)***	(3.02)***	(3.48)***
Professional	0.795	0.854	0.761	1.079
	(2.87)***	(2.95)***	(2.75)***	(3.25)***
Ln household Income	1.066	-	-	-
	(9.19)***	-	-	-
Owner	-0.137	-0.099	-0.126	-0.053
	(1.11)	(0.79)	(1.00)	(0.39)
Public Sector	0.050	0.030	0.106	0.092
	(0.39)	(0.22)	(0.81)	(0.68)
Private Sector	-0.308	-0.324	-0.318	-0.344
	(2.89)***	(2.95)***	(2.81)***	(2.93)***
Other Property	0.216	0.169	0.161	0.061
	(2.03)**	(1.53)	(1.46)	(0.51)
Car ownership	0.404	0.392	0.367	0.486
	(3.62)***	(3.22)***	(3.16)***	(4.05)***
Ln household Income Second Quartile	-	0.575	-	-
	-	(3.98)***	-	-
Ln household Third Quartile	-	0.950	-	-
	-	(6.05)***	-	-
Ln household Income Fourth Quartile	-	1.604	-	-
	-	(9.87)***	-	-
Ln Monthly Salary	-	-	1.012	-
	-	-	(8.62)***	-
Ln Monthly Salary Second Quartile	-	-	-	0.537
	-	-	-	(3.55)***
Ln Monthly Salary Third Quartile	-	-	-	0.736
	-	-	-	(4.56)***
Ln Monthly Salary Fourth Quartile	-	-	-	1.189
	-	-	-	(6.02)***
Constant	-3.628	5.932	-2.989	5.812
	(3.51)***	(19.34)***	(2.84)***	(16.87)***
F-test	34.23	26.36	28.74	21.51
R^2	0.60	0.59	0.57	0.53
N	329	330	317	330

** $p < 0.05$; *** $p < 0.01$, *$p < 0.10$

Source: Authors' Computation

From Table 6.3, it is first observed that total debt repayment rises with age. The same result holds for debt repayment as a share of income. It can be postulated that those in the age bracket above 60 face higher levels of debt repayment as the coefficient of this age category is much larger and statistically significant relative to other age brackets. In addition, the same positive link between family size and total debt repayment is noted where a larger family size implies more debts and higher repayments. Further, the positive link between education and total debt repayment is observed with a greater magnitude of the coefficients on the tertiary education variable and the professional qualifications dummy. The positive relationship between income and total debt repayment is robust and the magnitude of the coefficient is higher for higher income categories implying that higher income groups tend to have higher debt burden and greater debt repayments. In terms of assets ownership, having a car is also positively and significantly related to total debt repayment of the household. Gender, marital status and ownership of other properties are not statistically significant.

Table 6.4. Regression Results of Debt Behavior of Mauritian Households (Total Debt Repayment as a Share of Income as Dependent Variable)

	lndebtrepayincome			
Age 30 to 39	0.534	0.545	0.546	0.550
	(2.90)***	(3.07)***	(2.91)***	(2.96)***
Age 40 to 49	0.549	0.545	0.574	0.553
	(3.06)***	(3.17)***	(3.19)***	(3.11)***
Age 50 to 59	0.387	0.392	0.443	0.415
	(2.09)**	(2.19)**	(2.38)**	(2.27)*
Age 60	1.004	1.019	1.039	1.028
	(4.28)***	(4.47)***	(4.57)***	(4.46)***
Male	0.003	0.015	0.024	0.012
	(0.03)	(0.15)	(0.23)	(0.12)
Family Size - 4	0.096	0.114	0.136	0.115
	(0.79)	(0.93)	(1.11)	(0.93)
Family Size - 5	0.352	0.376	0.392	0.392
	(2.39)**	(2.49)**	(2.59)***	(2.63)***
Married	-0.147	-0.142	-0.131	-0.153
	(1.03)	(1.01)	(0.94)	(1.07)
Primary Education	0.536	0.526	0.493	0.511
	(2.05)**	(1.99)**	(1.89)*	(1.98)**
Secondary Education	0.550	0.532	0.549	0.537
	(2.41)**	(2.29)**	(2.38)**	(2.36)**
Tertiary Education	0.652	0.626	0.697	0.659

Table 6.4. (Continued)

	lndebtrepayincome			
	(2.88)***	(2.72)***	(3.02)***	(2.89)***
Professional	0.649	0.601	0.761	0.667
	(2.40)**	(2.21)**	(2.75)***	(2.43)**
Ln household Income	0.218			
	(1.85)*			
Owner	-0.155	-0.142	-0.126	-0.136
	(1.26)	(1.14)	(1.00)	(1.08)
Public Sector	0.110	0.122	0.106	0.120
	(0.85)	(0.96)	(0.81)	(0.92)
Private Sector	-0.278	-0.281	-0.318	-0.294
	(2.46)**	(2.55)**	(2.81)***	(2.64)***
Other Property	0.154	0.151	0.161	0.143
	(1.42)	(1.38)	(1.46)	(1.28)
Car ownership	0.307	0.285	0.367	0.323
	(2.65)***	(2.42)**	(3.16)***	(2.84)***
Ln household Income Second Quartile		-0.001		
		(0.01)		
Ln household Third Quartile		0.070		
		(0.42)		
Ln household Income Fourth Quartile		0.347		
		(2.07)**		
Ln Monthly Salary			0.012	
			(0.10)	
Ln Monthly Salary Second Quartile				0.087
				(0.58)
Ln Monthly Salary Third Quartile				0.069
				(0.43)
Ln Monthly Salary Fourth Quartile				0.238
				(1.34)
Constant	-4.854	-2.856	-2.989	-2.873
	(4.52)***	(9.75)***	(2.84)***	(9.87)***
F-Test	9.26	8.94	8.55	8.27
R^2	0.29	0.30	0.28	0.29
N	316	317	317	317

* *$p < 0.05$; *** $p < 0.01$, *$p < 0.1$
Source: Authors' Computation

In addition, Table 6.4 shows the findings where the dependent variable is debt repayment as a share of income. Regardless of whether households have "over-borrowed", the larger stock of household debt and debt repayments has important implications on the family. These consequences include the increased sensitivity of the household sector to fluctuations in income, interest rates, house prices and external shocks. The largest and most significant negative shock to household income is unemployment. Greater household indebtedness and higher debt service levels will heighten the sensitivity of households to a rise in unemployment (Debelle, 2004). Hence, households with debt will find it more difficult to maintain their mortgage payments through a period of unemployment, and hence will be more likely to default. Households may also be surprised in later years by the proportion of income still required to service their debt, and hence have lower than desired consumption (Debelle, 2004). Our findings reveal that households in the higher income categories face higher share of debt repayment to income.

Over Indebtedness of Mauritian Households

Table 6.5 shows the regression results for equation (5) where we establish a range between 20 to 40 per cent to capture the percentage of over-indebted households in the sample. Using logistic regression technique, it is noted that those households aged 60 and above are likely to be more over-indebted relative to those in the lowest age category. The positive and statistically significant coefficient for those households aged 60 and above is greater relative to all age brackets, revealing that elderly families tend to be more over-indebted. As for gender, female headed households tend to be more over indebted with a higher debt to income ratio relative to their male counterparts. In fact, in Mauritius life expectancy is relative higher for female than male and as such many women find themselves in a difficult situation when they need to cater for household needs at a later stage of their life. The results further show that those working in the public sector are less likely to be over indebted compared to those working in semi-public institutions. Besides, those households with a family size of 5 members and above are also more likely to be overindebted. This is in line with previous studies, where the larger the family size, the greater the expenses and the higher the likelihood of acquiring debts. The ownership of other properties also increases the risk of the Mauritian household to have high total debt to income ratio as postulated by the positive and statistically significant coefficient where debt lies in the range of 20 to 25 per cent of income.

Table 6.5. Regression Results of Debt Behavior of Mauritian Households (Total Debt as a Share of Income at Different Levels as Dependent Variables)

Total Debt as a share of Household Income	*40%*	*35%*	*30%*	*25%*	*20%*	*Logit (40%)*
Age 30 to 39	0.215	0.254	0.235	0.189	0.200	0.994
	(3.87)***	(4.33)***	(3.88)***	(1.91)*	(2.05)**	(28.25)***
Age 40 to 49	0.233	0.235	0.236	0.187	0.210	0.997
	(4.09)***	(4.06)***	(3.94)***	(1.89)*	(2.15)**	(29.54)***
Age 50 to 59	0.167	0.18	0.188	0.101	0.089	0.998
	(3.04)***	(3.25)***	(3.24)***	(1.03)	(0.92)	(26.77)***
Age 60+	0.250	0.277	0.282	0.215	0.208	0.990
	(3.42)***	(3.72)***	(3.67)***	(1.99)**	(1.93)*	(27.16)***
Male	-0.123	-0.119	-0.11	-0.109	-0.143	-0.096
	(2.20)**	(2.06)**	(1.85)*	(1.80)*	(2.33)**	(2.37)**
Family Size - 4	-0.008	0.012	0.025	0.046	0.051	0.003
	(0.14)	(0.20)	(0.41)	(0.72)	(0.80)	(0.07)
Family Size - 5	-0.001	0.031	0.117	0.148	0.181	0.009
	(0.02)	(0.40)	(1.46)	(1.83)*	(2.24)**	(0.18)
Married	-0.005	0.004	-0.072	-0.097	-0.074	-0.002
	(0.07)	(0.05)	(0.97)	(1.26)	(0.96)	(0.06)
Primary Education	-0.08	-0.077	-0.073	-0.105	-0.088	-0.049
	(0.61)	(0.58)	(0.55)	(0.79)	(0.65)	(0.75)
Secondary Education	-0.069	-0.057	-0.032	-0.056	-0.028	-0.040
	(0.59)	(0.49)	(0.27)	(0.48)	(0.24)	(0.63)
Tertiary Education	-0.074	-0.068	-0.021	-0.04	-0.013	-0.042
	(0.62)	(0.58)	(0.17)	(0.32)	(0.10)	(0.68)

Total Debt as a share of Household Income	*40%*	*35%*	*30%*	*25%*	*20%*	*Logit (40%)*
Professional	-0.072	-0.016	0.029	0.053	0.021	-0.041
	(0.52)	(0.11)	(0.19)	(0.35)	(0.14)	(0.54)
Ln household Income Second Quartile	-0.072	-0.06	-0.044	-0.041	-0.014	-0.048
	(1.16)	(0.95)	(0.69)	(0.64)	(0.22)	(1.23)
Ln household Third Quartile	-0.084	-0.06	-0.05	-0.071	-0.07	-0.053
	(1.21)	(0.85)	(0.69)	(0.96)	(0.93)	(1.32)
Ln household Income Fourth Quartile	-0.047	-0.022	0.01	0.025	0.046	-0.033
	(0.61)	(0.27)	(0.12)	(0.29)	(0.53)	(0.72)
Owner	-0.131	-0.131	-0.134	-0.127	-0.125	-0.105
	(2.16)**	(2.12)**	(2.14)**	(2.02)**	(1.95)*	(2.41)**
Public Sector	-0.122	-0.085	-0.092	-0.047	-0.048	-0.066
	(2.12)**	(1.40)	(1.43)	(0.71)	(0.69)	(1.90)*
Private Sector	-0.182	-0.18	-0.184	-0.184	-0.217	-0.120
	(3.54)***	(3.44)***	(3.39)***	(3.35)***	(3.85)***	(3.55)***
Other Property	0.089	0.079	0.105	0.176	0.156	0.074
	(1.42)	(1.25)	(1.57)	(2.56)**	(2.22)**	(1.58)
Car ownership	-0.031	-0.068	-0.065	-0.063	-0.035	-0.026
	(0.61)	(1.25)	(1.16)	(1.11)	(0.60)	(0.75)
Constant	0.424	0.375	0.386	0.471	0.458	_
	(3.40)***	(3.01)***	(2.97)***	(3.16)***	(3.08)***	_
R2	0.12	0.10	0.11	0.13	0.14	0.110
N	393	393	393	393	393	393

* *$p < 0.05$; *** $p < 0.01$, *$p < 0.1$

Source: Authors' Computation

Chapter 7

RECOMMENDATIONS AND CONCLUSION

Sanjeev K. Sobhee

REVIEW OF THE FINDINGS

This book is about household indebtedness in the context of Mauritius as an Upper Middle Income Economy. It attempts to shed more light on the causes of such indebtedness and the factors that contribute to over-indebtedness. The study has used mixed methods to address the research questions with the main aim of better understanding the evolution of high indebtedness, as has been pointed out by other researchers, published reports and the media in Mauritius. Moreover, the study has, at the same time, helped to provide relevant policy recommendations; in trying to ease the economic and social life-style of current as well as future generations.

Along the lines of existing conventional wisdom, while it has been established that higher income breeds higher indebtedness, it was observed that debt level varies differently across different income groups. It has been reported that consumers as households were found to be more indebted when their income is low. In a similar vein, since educational attainment is found to be correlated with income, the more educated the respondents, the higher the amount of debt contracted. Out of the total number of households surveyed, 83 per cent were found to be indebted. The highest proportion of debt contracted by individual borrowers pertains to the banking sector followed by commercial enterprises through hire purchase credit.

A investigation into the nature of loans contracted has enabled the researchers to confirm that much indebtedness occurs due to housing loans, followed by credit purchases of durable goods, loans contracted for the purchase of a vehicle and loans taken to finance a marriage (for self or akin or a relative). It was also found that debt level against age follows an N-shaped curve; whereby, the highest number of borrowers was found in the age group 30-39 followed by that of 40-49. A notable feature of the sample is that more borrowers were found in the age group above 60 than those in the age group of 50-60. In particular, a large proportion of retirees were thus found to hold debt.

Yet another feature of the study was to assess the degree of over-indebtedness; and to achieve this objective, four indicators were hypothesized and empirically tested. These were arrears in paying utility bills, servicing debt beyond a threshold of 40% of household income, cancellation of credit cards by banks and reporting on the difficulty in meeting current household's monthly expenses. While the benchmark for indebtedness is normally reached when a household services more than 40% of her income as debt, it was found that 5.5per cent of the sample lends support to this phenomenon. Actually, one third of the sample reported that they have arrears in settling utility bills. It was also found that monthly arrears in paying utility bills are inversely related to higher income. Most of the debt contracted is found to be driven by male households who are also found to be more severely indebted, if not over-indebted. In fact, quite a few households have reported that they had their credit cards seized because they could not honor their repayment terms.

There is strong evidence of 'demonstration effect' among Mauritian consumers in their spending habits as well as the demand in loans. For instance, in the purchase of a vehicle, which has become a necessity especially among households found in higher income brackets and for the purchase of durable goods (electronic goods and equipment). Households of different income categories were found to have borrowed money for particularly the same purpose with a lower degree of variability among them.

From a macroeconomic point of view, the rise in income inequality and the rise in the lowest quartile of income earners, as revealed by this study, indicate that family budget constraints have become more binding especially for low income and middle income groups with more than 3 dependents. Rises in Average Propensity to Consume (APC) and Marginal Propensity to Consume (MPC) do show that consumption expenditure has increased faster than income earned over the past decade. The increases in proportion of expenditure on 'Food and non-alcoholic beverages', 'Transport' and 'Housing and Utilities', reveal that rising cost of living makes it worse for an average indebted household to service her debt consistently. With the exception of the years 2008/09, over the years following the global financial crisis, household credit has remained fairly stable.

SOME POLICY IMPLICATIONS

The fact that many households have reported difficulties in servicing debt, especially on loans contracted for the purchase of durable goods, they must indeed be financially educated to avoid becoming defaulters.. It has been found that they may have arrears of payment in their utility bills, have their credit cards seized and experience difficulty in meeting current household expenses, especially foodstuffs. Such tendency would indicate the inability of indebted households to properly plan and manage their debt. This would require sensitization of all borrowers and especially economically-disadvantaged people to avoid an acute debt crisis situation. Concerned authorities may provide and support targeted programmes through a broad range of media to achieve such objective. As such, it would be expected that households would become more financially literate, responsible and would effectively manage their debt, irrespective of age and income.

The fact that many indebted households have reported that the main causes of their financial crisis pertain to asset acquisition such as purchase/construction of a house, hire purchase credit and the purchase of a vehicle, it is important that consumers do a proper assessment of their financial status periodically so that they could judge for themselves whether they would be able to commit to the purchase of several such assets concurrently or consecutively. It is recommended to borrowers, especially those who are more financially constrained, to review their financial status prior to committing themselves to over-indebtedness.

In addition, it has also been reported that households are indebted because of health care expenditures. Here again, it would be worthy to track whether households who are in their youth or middle age do take advantage of medical insurance schemes that are now provided and facilitated in both public and private sectors. Employees have to subscribe to these to avoid contingencies involving high sums at a later stage in their life or as and when they need to cover substantial medical expenses for themselves or members of their family. To a large extent, this would reduce the demand for loans contracted for medical treatment especially among retirees and for any category of employee.

Risks assessment by debt holders is yet something that has to be taken care of with more than a pinch of salt. As it is, there are many risks that are associated with the expected stream of income against which households tend to borrow. Such stream of income involves major fluctuations, uncertainties and the risks of income drifting too low. Concerned households must thus ensure that such risks are properly factored in prior to committing themselves to the purchase of capital assets. As such, households have to be more forward looking in terms of the demographic evolution of the family which is often overlooked and ultimately tightening the budget constraint of the borrower. There are common expenses such as educational loans, newly born members, marriage of a family member, extension and renovation of the house that are often linked to demographic changes and overlooked in the decision making process when a loan is borrowed.

It is further recommended that households gather more information before actually committing their income and demand for loans for purposes that involve substantial investment, such as, house construction, extension of property, purchase of vehicles and household equipment. They have to really shop around to find whether they could ease their potential debt by informing themselves more about terms and conditions of payment of loans and hire purchase conditions as well as the different financial products that they can have recourse too before actually committing themselves financially.

Coming now to what the authorities can do, it can be recommended that a credit bureau be created to advise customers or potential borrowers on over-indebtedness, credit management, customer education and risks and uncertainties associated with credit. This organization could be an important organ as a customer credit regulatory bureau to ensure that clients of the financial sector as well as commercial enterprises are well aware of all the financial implications and risks associated with borrowings, overdrafts, hire purchase and rescheduling of loans. It is expected that such an entity should act as an independent advisor and report cases of irregularity as well to the authorities (Bank of Mauritius or Financial Services Commission).

Most of the respondents in the survey have indicated that they have substantial amounts of housing loans and servicing these becomes very difficult because of specific reasons such as demographic changes, lower incomes, rise in cost of living, increase in interest rates, amongst others. It is highly recommended that government provides more financial assistance to certain income categories such as the first and second income quartiles which are indebted due to housing loans. Special schemes could be provided to them for acquisition of land, for example, at a subsidized rate, such that this could ease their borrowing costs from banks for construction purposes.

Since there is a high proportion of households who have stated that they have become indebted and over-indebted due to hire purchase as they find it difficult ultimately to meet their regular monthly expenses, including food items and utility bills, it is high time that the authorities review the hire purchase terms and conditions provided by various commercial enterprises. Very often, it becomes easier to acquire a durable product such as an electrical appliance without having to spare a lot of money during the purchase, but over the long term, the purchaser is overburdened with high interest obligations and an increasingly long period over which the credit has been spread. The desire to acquire durable goods is an illusion as its cost is perceived as being low. More screening is thus advised before allocating credit facilities to customers.

It is implied in the rising propensity to consume, observed over the last decade, that households have become indebted across years because of monetary factors related to inflation and interest rates. Higher inflation distorts the purchasing power of consumers making it more difficult for debtors to service their debt promptly. On the other hand, the spread between the savings rate and the lending rates of commercial banks discourages households from savings and building up enough bank balance to partially fund a capital project. With more savings, the purchase of land or construction of a house or purchase of housing equipment under hire purchase would thus be negotiated under more favorable terms and conditions. On the other hand, borrowers are urged to pay high interest on long term secured loans exacerbated with a matching and costly insurance premium to back such loans. It is a matter of concern for government to play a more preponderant role in revising housing and similar schemes provided by financial institutions to facilitate access to credit for personal loans in a near future.

REFERENCES

ABID, L., Zouari, D. & Zouari – Ghorbel, S. (2012). "Household Indebtedness in Tunisia," *E3 Journal of Business Management and Economics*, Vol. *3*(10), pp. 341 – 350.

Alessie, R., Hochguertel, S. & Weber, G. (2005) "Consumer Credit: Evidence from Italian Micro Data", *Journal of the European Economic Association*, Vol. *3*, pp. 144 – 178.

Attfield, Clifford, L. F. & Browning, Martin, J. (1985). "A Differential Demand System, Rational Expectations and the Life Cycle Hypothesis," *Econometrica, Econometric Society*, vol. *53*(1), pages 31-48

Bank of Mauritius, (2011). "Financial Stability Report". Mauritius

Bank of Mauritius, (2012). "Financial Stability Report". Mauritius

Bank of Mauritius, (2014). "Financial Stability Report". Mauritius

Bank of Thailand Report, (2013).

Balmer, N., Pleasence, P., Buck, A. & walker, H. C. (2006). Worried sick: the experience of debt problems and their relationship with health, illness and disability. *Social Policy and Society*, *5*(01), pp.39-51.

Barba, A. & Pivetti, M. (2009). Rising household debt: Its causes and macroeconomic implications—a long-period analysis. *Cambridge Journal of Economics*, *33*(1), pp.113-137.

Barnes, S. & Young, G. (2003). "The rise in US household debt: assessing its causes and sustainability", Bank of England Working Paper, no 206.

Berthoud, R. & Kempson, E. (1992) *Credit and Debt: the PSI report*, London: Policy Studies Institute.

Bertola, G., Hochgurtel, S. & Koeniger, W. (2005). "Dealer Pricing of Consumer Credit", *International Economic Review*, Vol. *46*, pp. 1103 – 42.

Betti, G., Dourmashkin, N., Rossi, M. & Yin, Y. (2007). "Consumer over-indebtedness in the EU: measurement and characteristics", *Journal of Economic Studies, 34*(2), 136-156

Betti, G., Dourmashkin, N., Rossi, M. C., Verma, V. & Yin, Y. P. (2001). "Study of the Problem of Consumer Indebtedness: Statistical Aspects". *Commission of the European Communities*, Directorate-General for Health and Consumer Protection, Commission of the European Communities, Brussels.

Bloxham, P. & Kent, C. (2009). Household indebtedness. *Australian Economic Review*, *42*(3), pp.327-339.

Bourdieu, (1979). La distinction. Critique sociale du jugement. Editions de Minuit.

Bridges, S., Disney, R. & Henley, A. (2006). "Housing wealth and the accumulation of financial debt: Evidence from UK households", in Bertola, G., Disney, R. and Grant, C., (eds) *The Economics of Consumer Credit*, Cambridge, Mass: MIT Press, pp. 135 – 180.

Bridges, S. & Disney, R. (2003). "Use of credit and arrears on debt among low income families in United Kingdom", mimeo, School of Economics, University of Nottingham.

Bridges, S. & Disney, R. (2004). "Use of credit and arrears on debt among low-income families in the United Kingdom", Fiscal Studies, *Institute for Fiscal Studies*, Vol. *25*(1), pp. 1 – 25.

Brown, S., Garino, G., Taylor, K. & Wheatley, P. S. (2005). "Debt and Financial Expectations: An Individual and Household Level Analysis", *Economic Inquiry*, Vol. *43*(1), pp. 100 – 20.

Browning, M. & Crossley, T. F. (2001). The life-cycle model of consumption and saving. *The Journal of Economic Perspectives*, *15*(3), pp.3-22.

Bryan, M., Taylor, M. & Veliziotis, M. (2010). "Over-Indebtedness in Great Britain: An analysis using the wealth and assets survey and household annual debtors survey", Institute for Social and Economic Research, University of Essex.

Butrica, B. A. & Karamcheva, N. S. (2013). "Does Household Debt Influence the Labor Supply and Benefit Claiming Decisions of Older Americans?" Boston College Center for Retirement Research Working Paper.

Cameron, S. & Golby, D. (1991). Personal debt crises: an economic approach. *International Review of Applied Economics*, *5*(3), pp.310-324.

Claessens, S., dell'ariccia, G., Igan, D. & Laeven, L. (2010). Cross-country experiences and policy implications from the global financial crisis. *Economic Policy*, *25*(62), pp. 267-293.

Cook, R. D. & Weisberg, S. (1983). "Diagnostics for heteroscedasticity in regression". *Biometrika*, *70*(1), 1-10.

Costa, S. & Farinha, L. (2012). "Households' Indebtedness: A Microeconomic Analysis based on the results of the Households' Financial and consumption survey". Financial stability report. Banco de Portugal.

Daniels, R. C. (2001). "Consumer Indebtedness among South Africa Households: A Descriptive Overview." Working paper. *Development Policy Research Unit, University of Cape Town.*, *01*(55).

Davydoff, A., Naacke, G., Dessart, E., Jentzsch, N., Figueira, F., Rothemund, M., Mueller, W., Kempson, E., Atkinson, A. & Finney, A. (2008). "Towards a common operational European definition of over-indebtedness, European Communities", Directorate-general for Employment, Social Affairs and Equal Opportunities European Commission.

Debelle, G. (2004). "Macroeconomic implications of rising household debt", *BIS working paper no. 153*.

Dornbusch, R., Fischer, S. & Startz, R. (2008). Macroeconomics. 9 th.

Disney, R., Bridges, S. & Gathergood, J. (2008). "Drivers of Over-indebtedness", Department of Business Enterprise and Regulatory Reform.

Dunn, L. F. & Mirzaie, I. A. (2013). "Determinants of Consumer Debt Stress: Differences by Debt Type and Gender", Working Paper Center for Human Resource Research.

Dusenberry, J. S. (1949). Income. Savings, and the Theory of Consumer Behavior Harvard University Press, Cambridge, MA.

Duygan-Bump, B. & Grant, C. (2009). "Household debt repayment behaviour: what role do institutions play?", *Economic Policy*, Vol. *24* (57), pp. 107 – 140.

dynan, K. & Kohn, D. L. (2007), "The Rise in U.S. Household indebtedness: Causes and Consequences", *Finance and Economics Discussion Series 2007-37*, Washington: Board of Governors of the Federal Reserve System.

Edwards, S. (2003). Debt relief and fiscal sustainability. *Review of World Economics*, *139*(1), pp.38-65.

Faruqui, U. (2008). "Indebtedness and the Household Financial Health: An Examination of the Canadian Debt Service Ratio Distribution". *Bank of Canada* Working paper., No. 2008, 46.

Ferreira, A. (2000). "Household over-indebtedness. Economic and Social Committee, Brussels: European Communities.

Finlay, S. M. (2006). "Predictive models of expenditure and over-indebtedness for assessing the affordability of new consumer credit applicants", *The Journal of the Operational Research Society*, *57* (6), 655-669.

Fisher, R. A. (1930). *The genetical theory of natural selection: a complete variorum edition*. Oxford University Press.

Flavin, M. A. (1984). "Excess Sensitivity of Consumption to Current Income: Liquidity Constraints or Myopia?", *National Bureau of Economic Research* Working Paper No. 1341, 1984.

Frankel, J. (2014). Mauritius: African success story. In *African Successes: Sustainable Growth, Volume 4*. University of Chicago Press.

Friedman, M. (1957). "A Theory of the Consumption Function", *Princeton: Princeton University Press.*

Gathergood, J. (2012). "Debt and depression: Causal links and social norm effects." *Economic Journal*, 122, 1094-1114.

Haas, O. J. (2006). "Over-indebtedness in Germany", Employment Section, Social Finance Program, Working Paper No. 44, International Labour Office: Geneva.

Haliassos, M. & Reiter, M. (2003). "Credit Card Debt Puzzles", mimeo, Conference on The Economics of Consumer Credit: European Experience and Lessons from the US, Finance and Consumption, EUI, Florence.

Hayashi, F. (1985). "Tests for Liquidity Constraints: A Critical Survey", NBER Working Paper 1720, Cambridge, Mass.

Herbert, A. & Kempson, E. (1995). "Water debt and disconnection", London: Policy Studies Institute.

Hubbard, R. G. & Judd, K. L. (1986). "Liquidity Constraints, Fiscal Policy, and Consumption", Brookings Papers on Economic Activity: 1.

Indian Ocean Times (2013). http://en.indian-ocean-times.com/Mauritius-75-of-households-according-to-the-association-for-the-protection-of-the-abused-borrowers-in-debt_a2337.html

Imam, P. & Kohler, R. (2010). Balance sheet vulnerabilities of Mauritius during a decade of shocks (No. 10/148). Washington, DC: International Monetary Fund.

Keese, M. (2009). "Triggers and determinants of severe household indebtedness in Germany", Ruhr Economic Paper, No. 150.

Kempson, E. (2002). "Over-indebtedness in Britain", London: Department Trade and Industry.

Kempson, E., Mckay, S. & Willitts, M. (2004), "Characteristics of families in debt and the nature of indebtedness", *DWP Research Report No. 211*, Leeds: HMSO.

Kim, Y. K. (2010). "The macroeconomic implications of household debt: An empirical analysis." Working Paper 1103, Trinity College.

Laibson, D., Repetto, A. & Tobacman, J. (2003). "Wealth accumulation, credit card borrowing and consumption-income co-movement", mimeo, Conference on The Economics of Consumer Credit: European Experience and Lessons from the US, Finance and Consumption, EUI, Florence.

Legge, J. & Heynes, A. (2009). Beyond reasonable debt: A background report on the indebtedness of New Zealand Families. *Social Policy Journal of New Zealand*, *35*, pp. 27-42.

Livingstone, S. M. & Lunt, P. K. (1992). Predicting personal debt and debt repayment: Psychological, social and economic determinants. *Journal of economic psychology*, *13*(1), pp. 111-134.

Lusardi, A. & Mitchell O. S. (2013). "Debt and Debt Management among Older Adults." Draft. Ann Arbor, MI: Michigan Retirement Research Center.

Macdonald, D. & Matier, C. (2016). "Household Indebtedness and Financial Vulnerability," Office of the Parliamentary Budget Officer. Ottawa. Canada.

Magri, S. (2002), "Italian Household Debt: Determinants of Demand and Supply", *Banca d'Italia, Temi di discussione del Servizio Studi, no. 454.*

Marmot, M., RY, C. D., Bumpass, L. L., Shipley, M. & Marks, N. F. (1997). "Social inequalities in health: Next questions and converging evidence", *Social Science and Medicine*, Vol. *44*(6), pp. 901 – 910.

May, O., Tudela, M. & Young, G. (2004). British household indebtedness and financial stress: a household-level picture. Bank of England Quarterly Bulletin, Winter.

Modigliani, F. (1986). "Life cycle hypothesis, individual thrift and the wealth of nations", *The American Economic Review*, Vol. *76*(3), pp. 297 – 313.

Modigliani, F. & Brumberg, R. (1954). Utility analysis and the consumption function: An interpretation of cross-section data. *Franco Modigliani, 1.*

Mori, (2004). "Over-indebtedness in Britain: A DTI report on the MORI Financial Services survey", available at: http://www.berr.gov.uk/ files/ file18550.pdf.

National Economic and Social Council, (2011). "Managing Indebtedness and Household Budgets for Better Living". NESC Report 19.

Oxera, (2004). "Are UK households over-indebted?", Commissioned by the Association for Payment Clearing Services, British Bankers Association, Consumer Credit Association and the Finance and Leasing Association.

Persson, M. (2009). "Household indebtedness in Sweden and implications for financial stability – the use of household-level data". Monetary and Economic Department, BIS Papers No. 46, Basel: Bank for International Settlements.

Poppe, C. (1999) "Risk Exposure to Payment Problems: Payment Problems Among Norwegians in the Nineties". In *Consumer Strategies in a Changing Financial Market*. 60th Anniversary Seminar October 1999. Oslo: SIFO.

Remolona, E. M. & Shim, I. (2008). "Credit derivatives and structured credit: the nascent markets of Asia and the Pacific". *BIS Quarterly Review*, June.

Rinaldi, L. & Sanchis-Arellano, A. (2006). "Household Debt Sustainability: What Explains Household Non-Performing Loans? An Empirical Analysis", *ECB Working Paper No. 570*, available at SSRN: http://ssrn.com/abstract=872528.

Roberts, R., Golding, J. & Towell, T. (1998), "Student finance and mental health", *The Psychologist (October)*, pp. 489 – 491.

Russell, H., Maître, B. & Donnelly, N. (2011). "Financial Exclusion and Over-indebtedness in Irish Households". Department of Community, Equality and Gaeltacht Affairs and Economic and Social Research Institute.

Schmidt-Hebbel, K., Serven, L. & Solimano, A. (1996). Saving and Investment: Paradigms, Puzzles, Policies. *The World Bank Research Observer*, *11*(1), pp.87-117.

Song, D. (2012). "The Cycle of Bubbles in Housing Prices by Analyzing Financial Intermediaries' Business Conducts of Home Loans", NHERI: Seoul, Korea.

Sobhee, S. K. (2009). The economic success of Mauritius: lessons and policy options for Africa. *Journal of Economic Policy Reform*, *12*(1), pp.29-42.

Stamp, S. (2006). "Research highlights need to focus on higher persistent debt risk to poor households", Dublin: Action on Poverty Today, Autumn 2006, No.14, pp. 12-13, Combat Poverty Agency.

Statistics Mauritius, "Household Budget Surveys, Various Issues".

Statistics Mauritius, "National Accounts, Various Issues". Ministry of Finance and Economic Development, Port Louis.

Swales, K. & Willitts, M. (2003). "Characteristics of large families." Information and Analysis Directorate, Department for Work and Pensions.

Subramanian, M. A. & Roy, M. D. (2001). Who Can Explain the Mauritian Miracle: Meade, Romer, Sachs, or Rodrik? (No. 1-116). International Monetary Fund.

Tandrayen-Ragoobur, V. & Kasseeah, H. (2012). "Poverty has a Woman's Face in Mauritius". *Journal of Social Policies and Development.*, available at: https://www.academia.edu/3788772/Poverty_has_a_Womans_Face_in_Mauritius.

Trigg, A. (2004). 'Deriving the engel curve: Pierre Bourdieu and the social critique of Maslow's hierarchy of needs', *Review of Social Economy*, Vol *62*(3), 393-406.

Tudela, M. & Young, G. (2005). "The determinants of household debt and balance sheets in the United Kingdom", Bank of England Working Paper no. 266.

Uppal, S. & Larochelle-Côté, S. (2015). Changes in wealth across the income distribution, 1999 to 2012. *Insights on Canadian Society*.

Veblen, T. (1922). The theory of the leisure class: an economic study of institutions. George, Allen Unwin, London (First published, 1899).

Watson, J. J. (2003). The relationship of materialism to spending tendencies, saving, and debt. *Journal of economic psychology*, *24*(6), pp. 723-739.

Webley, P. & Nyhus, E. K. (2001). "Life-cycle and dispositional routes into problem debt". *British Journal of Psychology*, *92*(3), 423-446.

Yao, J. Y., El-Maasry, G. Z., Khandelwal, P. & Sacerdoti, E. (2005). Mauritius: challenges of sustained growth. International Monetary Fund.

About the Authors

Name: Sobhee K. Sanjeev
Present Position: Professor
Academic Affiliation: University of Mauritius

Sanjeev K Sobhee is Professor of Applied Economics and Development Studies. His research areas include macroeconomics of the environment, sustainable development policies and the economics of climate change. Professor Sobhee has published extensively in internationally refereed journals and has consulted on projects for various international institutions: The World Bank, UNDP, UNEP, FAO, IOM and UNCTAD.

Name: Verena Tandrayen-Ragoobur
Present Position: Associate Professor
Academic Affiliation: University of Mauritius

Verena Tandrayen-Ragoobur is presently Associate Professor in the Department of Economics and Statistics at the University of Mauritius. Her research areas include international trade,, labour market, gender inequality and poverty. Her work relates essentially to countries of the African continent with main focus being on Sub Saharan Africa.

Name: Harshana Kasseeah
Present Position: Senior Lecturer
Academic Affiliation: University of Mauritius

Harshana Kasseeah is presently Senior Lecturer in the Department of Economics and Statistics at the University of Mauritius. Her research areas include finance and development with particular focus on small businesses and entrepreneurship, investigated from a gendered perspective. She has published in a number of international journals and has also completed several projects having a socio-economic dimension.

Name: Ruben Thoplan
Present Position: Lecturer
Academic Affiliation: University of Mauritius

Ruben Thoplan is a lecturer in Statistics at the University of Mauritius since August 2009. He holds a Master of Applied Statistics from the Macquarie University (Sydney), Australia. He is presently research active and his research interest covers the areas of Data Mining, and Time Series. With international experience in academia, Mr Ruben Thoplan has been a Statistics Tutor at the Sydney Institute of Business and Technology, Statistical Advisor and Research Assistant at Macquarie University before joining the University of Mauritius as lecturer. His research work was based on the modeling of spikes in the spot price of electricity for New South Wales.

INDEX

D

E

F

G

H

I

L

M

N

O

P

Q

R